Conflict Management - Organizational Happiness, Mindfulness, and Coping Strategies

Edited by
Francisco Manuel Morales-Rodríguez

Published in London, United Kingdom

Conflict Management - Organizational Happiness, Mindfulness, and Coping Strategies
http://dx.doi.org/10.5772/intechopen.110981
Edited by Francisco Manuel Morales-Rodríguez

Contributors
Albert Levis, Ana María Morales-Rodríguez, Francisco Manuel Morales-Rodríguez, Herbert Kanengoni, Jeffrey Gruenglas, Josh Hyatt, Martha Harunavamwe, Parul Acharya, Tomoko Kuniyoshi, Zohreh Hosseinzadeh

First published in London, United Kingdom, 2024 by IntechOpen
IntechOpen is the global imprint of INTECHOPEN LIMITED, registered in England and Wales, registration number: 11086078, 5 Princes Gate Court, London, SW7 2QJ, United Kingdom

British Library Cataloguing-in-Publication Data
A catalogue record for this book is available from the British Library

Additional hard and PDF copies can be obtained from orders@intechopen.com

Conflict Management - Organizational Happiness, Mindfulness, and Coping Strategies
Edited by Francisco Manuel Morales-Rodríguez
p. cm.
Print ISBN 978-0-85466-209-8
Online ISBN 978-0-85466-208-1
eBook (PDF) ISBN 978-0-85466-210-4

For EU product safety concerns:
IN TECH d.o.o., Prolaz Marije Krucifikse Kozulić 3, 51000 Rijeka, Croatia,
info@intechopen.com or visit our website at intechopen.com.

Meet the editor

Francisco Manuel Morales-Rodríguez has a Ph.D. in Psychology and a degree in labor sciences. He is a full professor at the University of Granada, Spain. He is active in research, coordinating and participating in innovation projects in education, training, and employment. He has published several books and articles in academic journals, as well as worked as a referee for journals and congresses. He is currently researching affective-sexual and gender diversities and coordinating the advanced innovation project "Transversal Education for Affective-Sexual, Gender and Corporal Diversities." Dr. Morales-Rodríguez was awarded one of nine research prizes from the General Foundation of the University of Málaga, Spain. He also received the William James Award for Psychopedagogical Innovation from the International Scientific Association of Psychopedagogy.

Contents

Preface

This book discusses conflict management, ethical considerations, and other relevant factors. It advances the knowledge of conflict management in the professional, work, and academic spheres.

The book includes seven chapters that are useful from a theoretical point of view and serve as reflective models that contribute to the improvement of conflict management, which is a daily requirement at many centers and institutions.

Chapter 1: "Conceptualizing Psychology as the Science of Conflict Resolution"

Chapter 2: "Ethical Considerations in Organizational Conflict"

Chapter 3: "Emotional Intelligence and Coping with Daily Stress in the Academic/Work Environment"

Chapter 4: "Changes in Mindfulness Attitude after Parent–Child Interaction Therapy Skills Acquisition: Comparison of Mindfulness Attitude before and after the Parent–Child Interaction Therapy 40 Hours Basic Training"

Chapter 5: "Conflicts in PK-12 Schools: Causes, Consequences and Management"

Chapter 6: "Harmony amidst Turmoil: Navigating Conflict with Mindfulness"

Chapter 7: "Technology Self-Efficacy and Mindfulness as Coping Strategies for Technostress in Hybrid Work Settings"

Francisco Manuel Morales-Rodríguez
Department of Developmental and Educational Psychology,
University of Granada,
Grenada, Spain

Chapter 1

Conceptualizing Psychology as the Science of Conflict Resolution

Albert Levis

Abstract

This essay introduces psychological concepts based on the scientific analysis of the creative process as a conflict resolution entity. This conceptualization was founded on Formal Theory's examining emotions as energetic entities and the unconscious, as manifested in creativity, as an energy and attitude transformation homeostatic mechanism. The theory evolved based on two observations: periodicity of a pattern and formal analysis of alternative cultural patterns. The unconscious therefore became a natural science, moral order measurable, qualifiable, graphically portrayable unit entity integrating art and science, psychology and morality. The benefit of this conceptualization is in its capacity to analyze the creative process utilizing a self-assessment, the Conflict Analysis Battery and playing Moral Monopoly, studying cultural stories reconciling religions. The scientific analysis of the conflict resolving unconscious transformed psychology into the Science of Conflict Resolution, the Moral Science. Accordingly organizational happiness examines social systems: the family, religions and ideologies as normative systems that are diagnosable, measurable, graphically portrayable, conflict resolving systems. Mindfulness, and Coping Strategies are examined in the context of a concise program of emotional education integrating art and science, using the self-assessment for self-discovery, and studying cultural stories examining the evolution of religions into the Moral Science.

Keywords: unconscious, psychology, conflict resolution, relational method, methodology, the creative process, personality typology, assessment, religions, scientific phenomena in behavior, energy, catharsis, moral values, emotional education, psychosynthesis, Moral Science, Science of Conflict Resolution

1. Introduction

The unconscious has been abandoned by contemporary psychology. Psychology has become an agnostic medical specialty, not interested in conflict, insight, and sociological changes. Psychology, as neuroscience, has been looking for answers studying the brain and utilizing medical interventions. This psychology focuses on illness rather than on wellness, diagnostic categories identify clusters of symptoms as stigmatizing illness diagnoses, assessments identify traits, not helping people to understand their personalities, and therapies address symptoms, not resolution of conflicts. Contemporary psychology is deprived of both basic science and the understanding of morality. Psychology's failure is manifested in the inability to educate students in achieving the three objectives of education: integration of art and science, self-knowledge and clarity of moral values [1].

Psychology's challenge in our times is in the scientific conceptualization of the unconscious. This is the conceptual focus of the Formal Theory of Behavior [2]. It advances a radically different position, presenting psychology as the exact Science of Conflict Resolution, the Moral Science.

The science begins by analyzing emotions as energetic and the unconscious as a conflict resolution energetic transformation mechanism.

The Formal Theory identified the unconscious as a natural science and moral order entity, conducting an energetic transformation consisting of a syndrome of emotions, a six-role state dialectic, leading to four types of conflict resolution social/moral adjustments, attitude changes. These are recognized as four relational modalities, a wellness personality typology. The wellness diagnoses account for pathology by distinguishing intensity of emotions. The unconscious as a natural science entity is measurable. A psychological self-assessment generates insights and guidance for changes. By understanding morality as conflict resolution, the Formal Theory recognizes religions as formally interrelated complementary discoveries of science that can be integrated into the new Moral Science.

The Moral Science Primer [1], presents multiple validations of Formal Theory's premise on the creative process as a conflict resolution energetic entity reflecting the unconscious. It is shown to integrate art and science, psychology and morality, religions among themselves, biology, sociology, and anthropology. This evidence validates the Formal Theory into the Moral Science.

Formal Theory's object of study has been the creative process; its method of study has been relational logic [3], as opposed to the currently used axiomatic or propositional method departing from arbitrary hypotheses to develop comprehensive models. Axiomatic statements vary as theories or stories, the relational method's alternative focus is on the universal structure, the plot of stories, identified as an energetic transformation, experienced emotionally and socially as conflict resolution. This emotional process accounts for the psychic origin of moral reasoning and also for pathologies.

The energetic and formal analysis of the creative process identified the unconscious as consisting of two entities: an emotional dialectic of six-role states, a syndrome, and an equilibrial transformation system of four types of conflict resolutions, the relational modalities. This premise is validated by identifying the six-role process syndromal structure of stories and the relational modality resolutions of the heroes of stories.

The Moral Science Primer [1] presents four types of validations of the theory:

1. Examining the art exhibits of the Museum of the Creative Process identifying the syndromal dialectic and the relational modalities in the analysis of multiple art exhibits [4];

2. Reviewing case studies using creativity for self-discovery again identifying the dialectic and the relational modalities structure of personal samples of creativity [5];

3. Reconciling religions as sanctifications of the four alternative types of conflict resolution, which thus may be integrated into the Moral Science.

4. A new validation has also been contributed by artificial intelligence, chat bots, through the analysis of any natural language text as consisting of the six-role syndromal process and the characters of texts diagnosed correctly as relational modalities [6].

The orderly formal analysis of conflict resolutions replaces the need for biological or neuroscientific attribution of psychopathology and the metaphysical attribution of morality. The shift of focus comprehending the structure of emotions as scientific energetic conflict resolution transformations following two phenomena of science leads to identifying meaning in software versus attributions to neuroscience, that is hardware, and theistic attributions to account for morality. The impact of this transformative research on psychology is like transforming astrology to astronomy, alchemy to chemistry and philosophy to clear principles of logic and physics. The Moral Science comprehends personal and sociological conflict choices founded on normative determinations thus placing ethics on the principles of the conflict resolution respecting laws of science.

2. Conflict Analysis, the Formal Theory of Behavior

The formal theoretical position studying emotions as energy and the creative process as a conflict resolution phenomenon evolved based on two observations: the first was of the recurrence of a pattern in the Greek creation stories. I puzzled over the cross-generational transmission of the pattern identifying the process as a syndrome consisting of six interrelated emotions (**Figure 1**) [7].

Stress, *Role Oppression*, was induced by a father, considering a son as a potential murderer, leading the father to oppress his son. The *Role Oppression* elicited in the son a *Role Assumption*, killing the father. The killing led to anxiety in the mind of the transgressor as *Anticipations of a Role Reversal*, being killed by one's children. This anxiety led to averting one's demise by a *Counterphobic Role Assumption*: killing one's children. This action provoked mothers to empower children to kill fathers, causing the hero's *Role Reversal*. Fathers were killed by their sons. One's demise, at the end of the cycle, elicited a *Compromise Role Assumption*: fathers cursing their children to be killed in their turn.

The cross-generational transmission of the six-role pattern accounted for the periodicity of the pattern. Upon the fourth repetition, Zeus swallowed Metis, his wife, averting being killed by her child; the child was Athena, who eventually was appointed as the goddess of Athens by her son, Erichthonius. The pattern was modified, leading to a conflict resolution, the creation of a religion, that of the Greek gods thriving on Olympus [4]. The conclusion from this observation was that religions are psychological sociological conflict resolution phenomena (**Figure 2**).

The second observation that inspired the Formal Theory was the relationship between four different cultural stories in dealing with power, or temptation; **Figure 1** identifies four interrelated types of dealing with the apple metaphor as alternative types of conflict resolution. The Greek apple inscribed 'to the fairest' generated competitiveness; it led to the Trojan War. The Judaic apple was forbidden; it led to cooperation. The Hindu apple was the sacred cow, which led men to austere asceticism, while the Aztec apple was a person's bleeding heart extracted from a victim, offered to the gods, thus eliciting maximal antagonism between parties. All these metaphors corresponded to alternative relational modalities, religions were normative

Figure 1.
The two observations that inspired the Formal Theory: periodicity and formality of alternative approaches to the apple metaphor as murals #1 and #6 the Sanctuary of Wisdom, at the Museum of the Creative Process.

Figure 2.
The six roles of the conflict resolution process as detected with the analysis of the Greek cosmogony pattern, illustrated above in mural #1 of the Sanctuary of Wisdom, at the Museum of the Creative Process.

institutions in formal relationship to each other. They embraced formally related types of resolving conflict. The apple metaphors were in formal relationship with each other. I recognized in the alternative choices three formal operations: reciprocity, negation and correlation, the formula of the formal operations restoring balance to the trays of a scale: I = RNC. (Identity is equal to the product of three operations: reciprocity, negation and correlation [7].

The first observation about periodicity was attributed to the transformation of emotions as energetic forms of the oscillating pendulum. The second observation pointing to formal alternatives between cultures represented the operations restoring the balance to the trays of a scale (**Figure 3**). The psychic scale's equilibrium could be restored with three operations: the first was the opposite behavior, removing the weight, transforming antagonism to cooperation, the second was the reciprocal change, placing a weight on the other tray of the scale; passivity was corrected by activity, and the third operation was shifting the weight on the fulcrum of the scale, the correlative change, the psyche evolving from alienation to mutual respect. The three operations corresponded to the syndromal emotional sequence summed up as attitude change, normative compliance, reduction of social conflict.

The two observations, periodicity and formality of equilibrial principles, led me to identify physical phenomena transforming energy as well as attitude as characteristics of the creative process. These were the operations underlying conflict resolution. The formal operations of the equilibrial scale accounted for the alternative types of conflict resolution as attitude change. The formal operations transformed a state of passivity to one of activity, one of antagonism to its opposite, cooperation, the third changed a state of alienation to one of mutual respect. The conclusion was that the unconscious consisted of a syndrome of six emotions: stress and response, anxiety

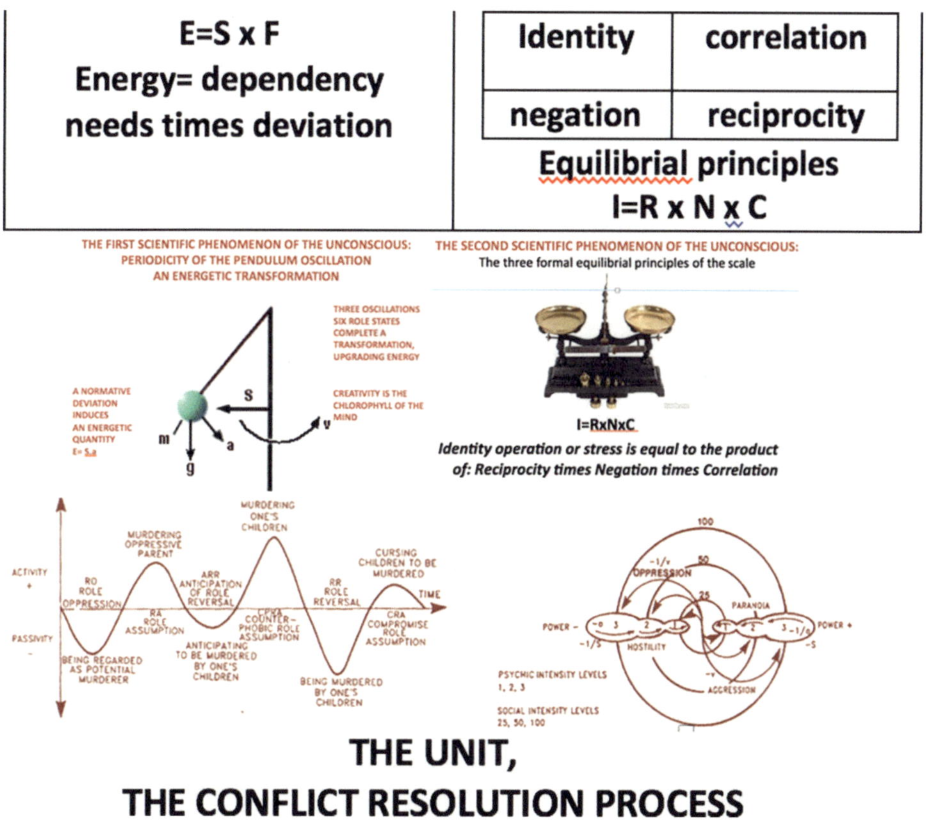

Figure 3.
The two phenomena of science corresponding to the two aspects of the unconscious, the syndromal six role process and the four relational modalities.

and defense, reversal and compromise, leading to four relational modalities: dominance versus subordinacy, in two variations: cooperative versus antagonistic.

The two phenomena of science conceptualized the unconscious as an energetic and attitude transforming entity beginning from a conflict, identified as passivity, antagonism and alienation, transformed to resolution as activity, cooperation and mutual respect. The attitude change restructured a person's disposition in the normative system. This energetic attitude transformation explained the adaptive and moral function of the unconscious. It conceptualized catharsis, the Greek word described by Aristotle as attitude change by identifying with the play's tragic hero [8], upon watching a Greek tragedy and experiencing an energetic modification. Psychic tension was released for the hero and for the audience, leading to catharsis, attitude change, an emotional sociological normative adjustment.

This scientific explanation clarified the unconscious as consisting of two components: 1. an energetic transformation syndrome of six-role states, six emotions, and 2. of the four relational modalities, the four types in resolving conflict, the diagnostic categories of wellness. Conflict resolution therefore corresponds to attitude change. The unconscious is defined then as a homeostatic function reducing psychic tension by modifying one's attitude. Homeostasis, conflict resolution, reduces psychic tension and increases social adjustment.

The unconscious transforming conflict related emotional energy to moral growth, conducts psychosynthesis, like chlorophyll's capturing solar energy in photosynthesis transforming it to physical growth. Religions have identified the alternative resolutions and sanctified them [1].

The equation of a psychological entity with the phenomena of science introduced constructs and formulas of science into the study of individual behavior as well as that of religions. This meant that the human unconscious as well as the cultural systems could be conceptualized with the constructs and formulas of the two scientific phenomena. Accordingly, the unconscious is graphically portrayable, it is measurable, and it leads to morality, conflict resolution as advocated by the respective religions.

The Moral Science's concepts represent a scientific breakthrough: unifying psychological disciplines through the scientific analysis of the creative process (**Table 1**).

The Formal Theory revamps psychology by introducing the study of the creative process as the object of formal analysis. It defines the unconscious as an energetic transformation, manifested as attitude change abiding by the constructs and formulas of two phenomena of science. This unconscious is graphically portrayable, it is qualifiable as wellness diagnoses; it is measurable with a self-assessment, generating

1. Epistemology Motivation is driven by the need to reduce psychic tension and improve social adjustment.	2. Diagnoses Personality typology consists of syndromes and four relational modalities, wellness and pathologies accounted for by a personality typology.
3. Assessment The Conflict Analysis Battery is a self-assessment that is didactic, diagnostic and therapeutic.	4. Morality Religions are normative institutions that identified and deified sequentially the four relational modalities. They evolved in abstraction and fairness, but have remained moral monopolies that may be integrated into the Moral Science.
italics added for emphasis.	

Table 1.
The Moral Science Primer's [1] four sections integrate the disciplines of epistemology, diagnosis, assessment and morality.

insights, and guidance for changes. It clarifies the evolution of religions as discoveries of the alternative types of conflict resolution. The study of the creative process is the core for a new science [9].

The two observations are illustrated in two murals of the Sanctuary of Wisdom of the Museum of the Creative Process (**Figure 1**). The one presents the six-role syndrome, the second the four modalities as choices in dealing with the apple metaphor. The observations conceptualize psychology and religions by identifying the study of the creative process as a scientific conflict resolution measurable and graphically portrayable mechanism representing the unconscious. The unconscious pattern as a natural science energy transforming becomes the unit order of the social sciences, placing psychology and morality on the analysis of the creative process as a natural science moral order phenomenon (**Figure 4**).

Epistemology: Epistemology identifies the unconscious by observing the creative process as a scientific conflict resolution mechanism consisting of an emotional six-role state dialectic leading to four alternative conflict resolutions. The process abides by two phenomena of science. It consists of a six emotions energy transforming dialectic guided by two innate formal principles, reciprocity and negation, leading to four alternative types of conflict resolution and a third formal operation correlation accounting for wellness versus pathologies.

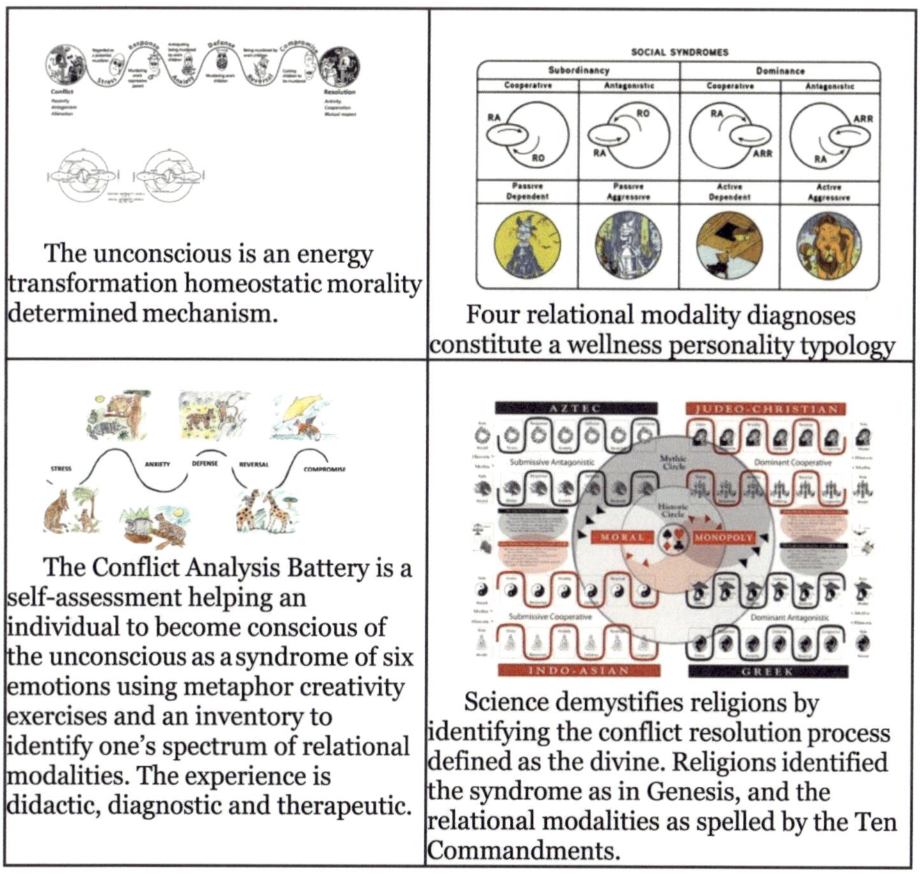

Figure 4.
The graphic representation of the unconscious as the unit integrating the four disciplines of psychology.

The Formal Theory defines the unconscious as a physiological processor of energy; the six-role process converts conflict energy into emotional and social adjustment or personal growth. The function of the unconscious process is homeostatic; it reduces unpleasant psychic tension by converting conflict or displeasure, maladjustment, through attitude change to order, restoring the rest state as normative relational adjustment. This energetic transformation unfolds as a syndrome, a constellation of emotions and behaviors existing as a circumscribed pattern consisting of six-role states: stress, response, anxiety, defense, reversal and compromise guided by three formal attitude-modifying formal operations to four alternative types of relational modalities.

Thus, the unconscious is a conflict resolution or moral order equilibrial phenomenon that has energetic, physical and formal, relational dimensions allowing its qualitative and quantitative measurement. The six-role state emotional continuum predictably unfolds upon any stressor as emotions and associations in one's mind as well as through interpersonal exchanges as three emotional oscillations guided by the three formal equilibrial operations seeking restoration of emotional balance as relief of tension.

The unconscious resolves conflicts as a syndrome guided by the three formal equilibrial operations of the restoration of balance to the trays of a scale. The three formal operations transform passivity to its reciprocal, activity, antagonism to its opposite, cooperation, and alienation to its correlative: mutual respect. Accordingly, the unconscious self-adjustment, the conflict resolution process, propels the individual one directionally to increased inner order, transforming stress energy into internalized and externally reinforced organization of behaviors along three formal operations each having a dichotomy.

Diagnosis: The Formal Theory innovates the field of diagnoses introducing two components in the analysis of diagnostic categories, syndromes and relational modalities. We identify four relational modalities unfolding as syndromes. These represent a personality typology, a new set of wellness diagnostic categories. Hence diagnosis is about identifying these two components of the unconscious. They are of psychodynamic nature accounting for pathogenesis, psychopathology and for psychotherapeutic interventions. The typology of wellness diagnoses as syndromes of four relational modalities is the relational alternative to the axiomatically established mental illnesses diagnoses, Diagnostic Statistical Manual 5 [9]. Of course, we recognize the medical nature of certain major psychopathologies independently of the relational psychodynamic make up of wellness diagnoses.

Diagnostic categories are determined by the innate formal distinctions. The operation of reciprocity introduces two distinctions: passivity versus activity; the operation of negation distinguishes the alternatives of cooperation and antagonism; these two formal operations lead to four conflict resolution modalities: the dominant and submissive relating; the formal operation of negation qualifies each one of the two reciprocal responses along the opposite directions of cooperation and antagonism. The four relational modalities are viewed relationally as power distinctions: dominance and subordinancy and attitude distinctions: as their cooperative and antagonistic variations. These four entities represent four wellness diagnostic categories. The psychic, emotional load, intensity of responses is addressed by the third operation: correlation, whose dichotomy is alienation versus mutual respect as high versus low psychic tension, wellness versus illness. The third formal operation allows the measurement of the individual's psychic tension, reflecting the intensity of conflict experienced as maladjustment or neuroticism. Dominant individual's pathology is in generating societal conflicts, while submissive individuals generate inner or psychic conflicts. Alienation, as increased intensity, may manifest with clinical symptoms as illness.

Assessment and therapy: The Conflict Analysis Battery [10] is a self-assessment leading to self-knowledge, becoming conscious of the unconscious and aware of the need to modify one's power, attitude and intensity of emotions. The assessment is deliverable online and as a workbook. It is introduced by an essay explaining the scope of the evaluation, then it combines a personality inventory, which is diagnostic with a set of creativity exercises, which are therapeutic. The inventory measures the modalities and also the psychic tension, pertaining to the intensity of conflicts experienced; it identifies relational modalities as qualitative distinctions, it also measures intensity of relational choices be those of dominance, submission, cooperation, and antagonism. The creativity tests, use metaphors to capture the six emotions of the syndromal structure of the process. They reconstruct the process, which generates insights and motivation for changes. The online delivery of the assessment is completed with a seven point report that is diagnostic and therapeutic.

The Conflict Analysis Battery helps the test taker to learn about the process, then to become conscious of the personal pattern, providing insights and guidance for relational changes. The assessment thus, is didactic, diagnostic and therapeutic. It represents a concise program of emotional education [11] that reconciles the humanities and the rigorous disciplines, delivers self-knowledge and clarity of moral values.

Morality: Religions are normative institutions seeking the reduction of personal and sociological conflicts. They command absolute authority on the faithful based on dogma. They do not allow critical analysis of the thought process. The science integrates religions as discoveries of the alternative ways of resolving conflicts by identifying progressively the three formal operations of resolving conflict: moderation, cooperation and mutual respect. The formal analysis of cultural stories integrates religions as moral monopolies into the Moral Science. Moral Monopoly is an educational game that recognizes religions as sanctifying the compliment of relational modalities in a progression of improving the family institution. Now religions reduced to particular conflict resolutions become accountable to the Moral Science determining the ultimate ethics. The public and the nations have now the rational analysis of morality as the charted paths to conflict resolution [12, 13].

Conceptual equivalences, **Tables 2** and **3**, wherein the unconscious process has been identified both by religions and psychoanalysis descriptively. These descriptions represent insights into science. Religions deified the moral authority of the unconscious, while psychological theorizing introduced clinical and philosophical explanations.

2.1 Organizational happiness: formal analysis of sociological systems

This section is an essay about the integration of psychological and sociological conceptual languages on the foundation that the unconscious creative process, a scientific conflict resolution phenomenon, is the integrative paradigm of both psychic and societal systems. The syndromal structure and relational modality function is the unit of the social sciences measuring individuals and organizations alike. The conceptualization of the unconscious as the unit order allows the integration of the disciplines of psychology: epistemology, wellness diagnoses, assessment, and therapeutic modalities with the study of cultural systems. Thus, all sociological phenomena such as the family, the organization, the culture, become measurable and graphically portrayable conflict resolution entities.

God	The unit of the creative process unconscious
Genesis	The six-role process and the formal operations leading to catharsis, energy transformation
The Ten Commandments	The formal operations of conflict resolution, moderation, cooperation and mutual respect
The four children asking 'what is special this night?'	Four relational modalities and syndromes
Celebration of the texts and the commandments	Moral education with Creativity and Power Management
Yom Kippur	The importance of introspection
Passover	Emotional education: assertiveness as the value system, confronting unjust authority empowered by principles of justice

Table 2.
Contrasting equivalent concepts of religion and the formal theory.

Observation	Hysteria	Periodicity of cosmogony
Object of study	Oedipus complex	The formal connection of the cultural metaphors of dealing with temptation.
Methodology	Propositional axiomatic method	Relational method
Unconscious	Defined as generating conflicts	Defined as reducing conflicts as adaptive attitude change
Motivation	Drives of libido and thanatos	Transforming conflict energy along three relational operations.
Energy	Cathexis and catharsis, the structural model	Emotions are energetic quantities. Catharsis is in the processing of emotions.
Structure	Id, ego, and superego	Six-role energetic transformation process, as continuity of action.
Relational principles	Defense mechanisms	Formal operations binding the six-role states: Identity = Reciprocity x Negation x Correlation
Graphics	Non-existing	Sine curve and concentric circles and ellipses with vectors
Diagnostic distinctions	Transference determined by formative experiences	Relational modalities are innate syndromal patterns of conflict resolution, personality types.
Developmental model	Oral, anal, phallic	Symbolic fixations upon traumatic experiences
Diagnostic therapeutic model	Couch, object relations, analysis of transference	Conflict Analysis Battery, combines a diagnostic inventory and therapeutic metaphors.
Morality	Moses as Oedipal dynamics	Morality is determined by the unconscious need of resolving conflicts
Civilizations	Philosophical analysis of discontents	Religions evolved as sanctification of the alternative ways of resolving conflicts.

Table 3.
Contrasting equivalent concepts of psychoanalysis and the formal theory.

In this section we introduce the conflict resolution process analysis of social systems utilizing two metaphors of sociological reality. The first is the symbolism of the American Flag as reflecting the two components of the unconscious in the analysis of social systems. The stars of this flag correspond to relational modalities in relationship with each other and the stripes of the flag correspond to syndromes of social systems examined. The second symbolic system is the deck of cards examining the formal interrelation of four suits as reflecting the four types of conflict resolution. The signs of the deck of cards indicate the relational modalities, while the suits represent the syndromes of the relational alternatives.

The flag presents three sections of the syndromal process to illustrate the shift from art to science, the cross-generational transmission and the versatility of the graphic portrayal of alternative types of conflict resolution.

Mural #2: The Flag of the United Metaphors of the World, **Figure 5**, shows that the Conflict Resolution Process is the common denominator of all social systems, indeed of all moral paradigms [4]. This flag celebrates the discovery that the unit process, the measurable entity of moral order by integrating the diversity of hitherto alienated belief systems into a familiar image that now is given physical and formal dimensions measuring religions and ideologies as graphically portrayable natural science phenomena [13]. The formal methodology reconciles the diversity of value systems as merely different approaches to conflict resolution. The unit of the unconscious is the structure underlying religions as well as those based on ideologies, such as economic paradigms of capitalism and communism. The revised American flag unites all religions and ideologies through the scientific interpretation of moral paradigms based on the measurability of the formal operations of power, attitude, and intensity and of their syndromal unfolding as a system of six role states. The flag illustrates the formal and natural scientific graphic composition of cultures as measurable syndromes and identifiable relational modalities (**Figure 6**).

Thus, the cultural metaphors placed on the power field in the context of each other's dimensions are given an accurate social/emotional formal qualitative and

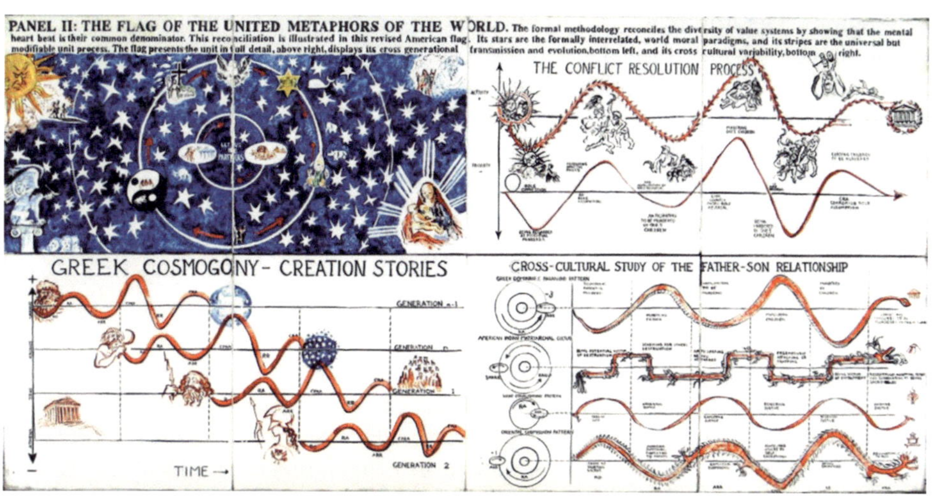

Figure 5.
The Flag of the United Metaphors illustrates the two components of the unconscious, the six-role syndromal process as stripes, and the relational modalities as stars placed in measurable parameters.

Figure 6.
The star section of the flag of the united metaphors presents religions and ideologies as having measurable dimensions.

quantitative description. I.e., the Judaic system, qualified as cooperative dominance (or assertiveness), is positioned on the dominant cooperative quadrant. Islam and Greece, characterized as valuing dominance and competitiveness, are placed on the second quadrant. Christianity and Buddhism characterized as the cooperative subordinacy choices are placed on the submissive cooperative third quadrant. The matriarchal submissive antagonistic modality is placed on the fourth quarter. Each normative system is then interrelated to each other as stars placed on suitable orbital positions and as stripes with different undulations. This implies that the constellations of the symbols of religions and cultures, the metaphors of the cultures of the world: the Cross, the Star of David, the Islamic Crescent and Star, the Oriental Yin-Yang, the bear brandishing the communist hammer and sickle, and the capitalist eagle, are all measurable alternative paths to conflict resolution [1, 13]. The four corners of the star section of the flag are occupied by four relational alternatives. The matriarchy and patriarchy on the left side indicate the antagonistic and polarized nature of the primitive religions. The Abrahamic religions on the right represent the dominant.

The striped section of the flag represents the syndromal process. It is the universal harmonic reflecting the graphic representation of the six-role process. The flag's stripes consist of variations of the Conflict Resolution Process, the common denominator, the atomistic unit of all moral metaphors, religions, and ideologies. The stripes of the flag are modifiable. There are three sets of stripes illustrating the unit, the unit's cross-generational transmission, and its variability.

- One set interprets the unit process from art to science as a syndrome of six-role states.

- The second set focuses on the cross-generational transmission of the pattern, as observed in the four consecutive generations of the Greek Cosmogony. This set of stripes interlock cross-generationally along with the six-role states transmitting the process. The interlocking of the four generations of the Greek Cosmogony determines the qualities of the transmitted pattern.

- The third set of stripes in the flag addresses the cross-cultural variability of the unit process as it is used to depict four principal cultural relational alternatives.

Integrating art and science	Greek cosmogony	Cross cultural study
The flag presents the unit in full detail as the evolution from art to science.	The flag displays the unit in its cross-generational transmission and evolution.	The flag shows the unit's cross-cultural variability.

Table 4.
The stripes illustrate the syndromal structure integrating art and science, cross-generation transmission and cross-cultural variability.

The modification of the sine wave eases the recognition of four pronounced variations corresponding to the four major cultures: the Greek sine curve is a snake, the Mexican Indian is a feathered serpent, the Judaic is a scroll, and the Oriental is a dragon. These four cultural paradigms illustrate four relational modalities or diagnostic categories of everyday cultural normative structuring of role relations (**Table 4**).

2.1.1 Three symbolisms of the game as the template of the unconscious

In parallel to evolving creation stories revamping norms in family relations, the public explored conflict resolution playing table games about family feuds. Chess is a game of family conflicts with clearly assigned roles for the members of the family as chess pieces. Another symbolic system, the deck of cards addresses four types of conflict resolutions between four cultures as representative royal families representing four cultures' alternative types of resolving conflicts as identified by the signs symbolic system. The four signs: the spade, the club, the diamond and the heart may be viewed as formally interrelated representing the four relational modalities. The signs structure the deck along formal distinctions.

- The colors red and black symbolize an opposite relationship: cooperation in red and antagonism in black. Accordingly spade and club in black, diamond and heart in red, may be viewed as symbolizing the opposites of antagonism and cooperation. Both the diamond and the heart as red denote cooperation.

- We may infer a reciprocal interrelation between the same-colored signs: The spade is an upside-down heart in black, needled by an arrow, portraying passivity. The club in black represents an explosion, activity, the reciprocal to the passivity state of the spade. Similarly, the diamond as straight lines, symbolizes containment, passivity, while the heart is a symbol of activity in a reciprocal position to the diamond.

- Both spade and diamond on the left quadrants reflect passivity and as opposite in color, reflect the opposites of antagonism and cooperation.

- Similarly, the heart and the club, both in mastery positions differ in color as the opposites of cooperation and antagonism.

- While the spade symbolizes conflict as passivity, antagonism, and alienation the heart symbolizes conflict resolution: mastery, cooperation and mutual respect.

- We may infer in the symbolism of the signs as a system, the continuity of emotional growth. Resolutions of conflict seem to evolve along the power and attitude formal distinctions from the conflictual spade to the resolved heart. Thus, the deck of cards brings together in one symbolic system the microcosm of the unconscious as seeking amelioration in resolutions of cultural relational alternatives.

2.1.2 Moral monopoly: analysis of the deck's gameboard retraces the evolution of religions as discoveries of the relational modalities

The card game template, **Figure 7**, presents metaphorically three features of the human unconscious: The suits, as a six-role process, the signs as the four relational modalities, and third, the systemic evolution of signs from the spade to the heart as the amelioration of the system. This structuring entails the evolution of attitudinal improvements based on scientific principles that may be used as the template of orderly sociological and also individual emotional developments.

Moral Monopoly is an educational game created as modification of the original deck of cards. The deck's four suits correspond to the four relational modalities. Each suit leads to a different type of conflict resolution. The alternatives are portrayed in the images illustrating the family dynamics between the key figures: kings, queens, and Jacks. Each suit with its set of cards represents the unfolding of the six-role conflict resolution process, as a syndrome modified by the signs.

- In rethinking the game of cards we divide the numbered cards into two stories: a mythic and a historic one. The mythic is about the culture's conflict and the

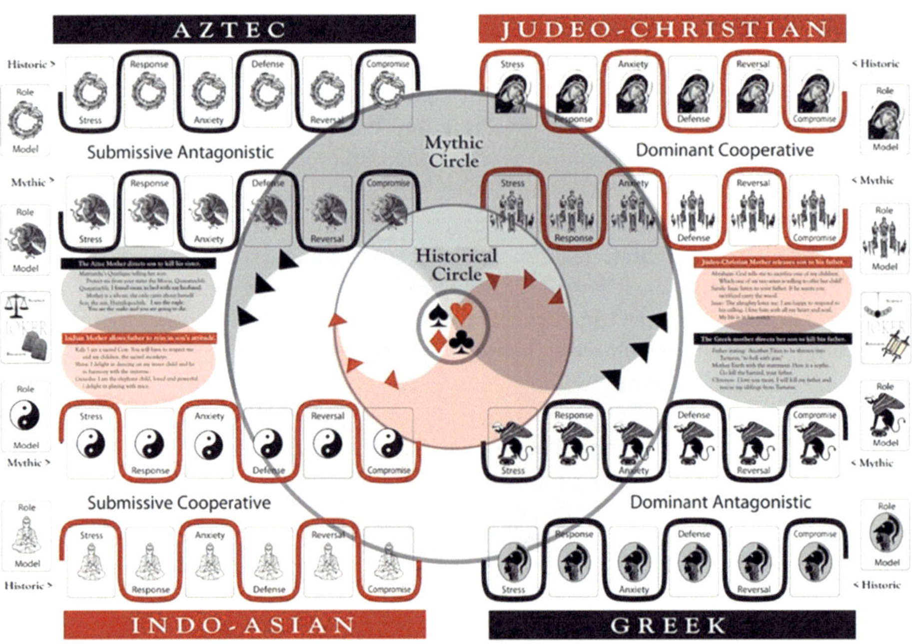

Figure 7.
The game-board of the card game as the template of the unconscious as captured by the evolving religions as discoveries of science.

historic about the conflict's resolution. The two stories have different face or family figures cards: The mythic story presents a conflict from the culture's mythology; the role model card portrays the image of family relations. The historical story is from the culture's documented record, the role model image illustrating the culture's dealing with power as in the apple of temptation metaphor, conveying the culture's relational modality. Thus, the new suit has two face cards representing the role models of the suit, and two sets of numbered cards as six-role state sequences. The relation between the two stories mythic and historic represents the culture's own conflict and type of resolution accomplishment.

- The four cultures of the card game are shown to be formally interrelated as reflected in the signs as the four types of conflict resolution. The symbols are formally related beginning from the spade as a black, upside-down heart that is poked, evolving to the upright red heart. The signs connect the four modalities into a cyclic evolutional dynamic.

- The two jokers are interpreted as representing the two phenomena of science underlying the orderly game of morality.

- The template of the new deck presents the two features of the game graphically: eight sine curves with undulations for the six episodes of stories, and two concentric circumferences with vectors clarifying the power and attitude dimensions of the four relational modalities. The figures of the signs, identifying the modalities are inserted diagonally on the template. The evolutional dynamic of the modalities is like the four seasons of the year, evolving sequentially toward optimizing conflict resolution in relational systems. They illustrate the references of periodicity in the cyclic improvement of conflict resolution. The power, attitude and intensity are graphically portrayable variables of the measurable relational operations. The six-role process is an emotional dialectic, the mental heartbeat, driven by the three formal operations, the steering mechanism as the moral compass.

The natural science dimensions of the game-board.

The game board is the map of the unconscious integrating society's relational modalities in the mode of a continuum of transformations. The game board is a field that has measurable dimensions determined by the two scientific phenomena pertaining to the analysis of the thought process:

- The Simple Harmonic Motion as a six-part pendulum oscillation as a sine curve is the structure of every one of the eight stories. The oscillations represent the emotional heartbeat as the six episodes resolving conflict transforming energy from chaos to order. The process corresponds to motivation as the driving force to reduce psychic tension, conflict energy, displeasure as psychic tension, and to increase pleasure as social adjustment.

- The laws of the equilibrial scale as a set of four formal attitude-changing equlibrial operations divide the board into four quadrants corresponding to the four relational modalities. The four relational modality dichotomies are presented graphically as a system of horizontal distinctions in power, as dominance versus subordinancy. Vectors within the circles present the opposites of cooperation as clockwise and antagonism as counterclockwise directions. The concentricity of circles and ellipses is used to indicate intensity differentials in mythic versus historical circles, reflecting alienation versus mutual respect within a system.

The relational modality distinctions of the normative totality make the game-board into the map of the unconscious as well as the map of measurable societal reality. In the game of Moral Monopoly the suits placed on the quadrants represent four religions as discoveries of the respective relational modalities.

2.1.3 The three features of the game-board: syndromes, relational modalities and ongoing healing

The four syndromal relational alternatives combined with the eight harmonics of the process provide the graphic dimensions of the societal unconscious (**Figure 8**). This structuring is of educational value. It represents becoming conscious of social order in continuity with psychological order. The map helps to retrace the evolution of the religions of the world as the continuum of the alternative ways the human mind has evolved historically in identifying alternative paths of resolving conflicts. Thus, the template identifies the three key scientific variables of the unconscious thought process.

The game presents the evolution of the religions/suits as formally connected relational modalities.

Reviewing what has been described above we identify in the composition of each of the eight stories representations of a family conflict resolutions (**Figure 9**). Each

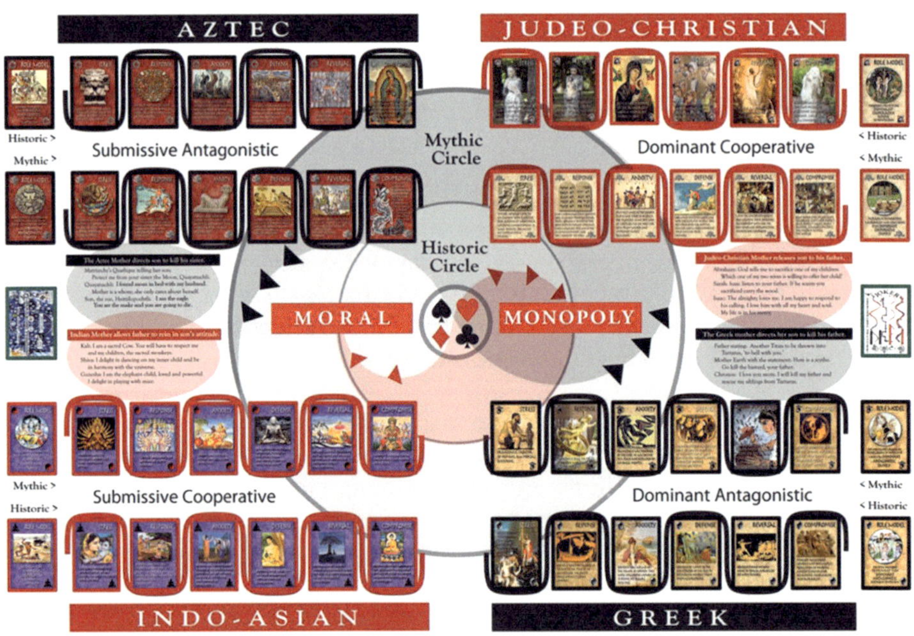

Figure 8.
Representation of the three scientific features of the unconscious unit conflict resolution process: The six-role state syndrome, the set of the four types of relational modalities as the four signs, and the sequencing of the four modalities as the periodicity of the self-improvement dynamic.

Figure 9.
A sample set of storytelling cards of the Greek culture representing patriarchy's contribution in improving family relations.

suit begins with a face card, here on the right of the image, illustrating the family configuration of roles. The ensuing cards present the episodes of stories as a conflict resolving process. Twelve cards of each suit present two stories, one from mythic times identifying the cultural conflict, the other, a story from historic times presenting the conflict's resolution.

The card game presents the self-improving, self-adjusting unconscious.

The deck uses the distinctions of the four signs: the spade, club, diamond and heart symbolizing the four alternative ways of resolving conflicts, the relational modalities, identifies four quadrants of the circle in the center of the game board. Each quadrant representing a relational modality their names are spelled out in the respective quadrant. The signs introduce the periodic transformation of relational modalities reflect the evolution of the optimization of the conflict resolution process. It is predictable like the seasons of the year. The signs are indicators of the periodicity. The sequencing of the four modalities is indicated as a periodic phenomenon. The red heart conclusion of one cycle becomes the spade departure for a new cycle of transformations. The game thus becomes a metaphor of the structure of the syndromal process, of its four relational modalities, and also of the evolution of the modalities of conflict resolution as a system that automatically progresses to self-improvement.

The story cards on the orderly template of the game board, establish the formal structure of the deck along the three components of the unconscious; they establish the psychological correspondence of stories to the scientific variables of the template and reflect the order provided by the psychological science to the analysis of sociological systems. Each culture exemplified by two stories, the eight stories reflect how religions evolved, improving the family institution from matriarchy to patriarchy, to asceticism and monotheism. The players examine the formal attributes of each cultural story beginning from the antagonistic Aztec, then the Greek culture, then the cooperative Indian, and Judaic variations.

The signage of the suits, spade to heart, reflect symbolically incremental effectiveness. The modalities evolve, improving relations in the family along the signage from the black upside-down heart of the spade, to the black explosive club, through the red diamond to the upright red heart.

The compounded image features the four suits dividing the power field into four quadrants for each of the four relational modalities; these are then populated by the stories of the four cultures presented as harmonics for each of the cultural stories. The game-board illustrates the self-improving moral unconscious encompassing all religions as an orderly progression improving family relations redefining the divine. According to the imagery, religions are integrated as complementary discoveries of the Moral Science, which clarifies the six-role process evolving along the three attitude-changing principles of conflict resolution. The cultures evolved seeking mastery, cooperation, and mutual respect. The Moral Monopoly board then, as the map of the unconscious, bridges science and psychology into the Moral Science. The game allows the scientific interpretation of religions as metaphors of an organic system of interrelated self-improving conflict resolutions. The study of cultures is relevant in the training of employees of an organization as a model of ongoing emotional growth process putting resolution of conflicts in a long-term evolutional perspective.

2.2 Mindfulness, and coping strategies

2.2.1 Introducing a concise program of emotional education

The public needs to be emotionally prepared in dealing with the dilemmas of everyday life. How can the individual be prepared to deal with psychological and sociological realities? The individual needs an emotional education in handling responses to stressors be those caused by inner conflicts or external such as dealing with the family, the nation, the city, and multiplicity of moral systems, religions? The individual needs help in interacting within the contemporary organizational and political systems; especially police officers and soldiers need training in dealing with armed conflict, dealing with personal feelings, traumas, aggressions, guilt for inflicting death, and suffering losses through death of comrades, dealing with suicidal thinking. More servicemen die from inner conflicts than from combat. The learning program should educate the person about oneself, and also about understanding alternative normative systems.

Social systems have an etiquette, norms of conduct, such as dealing with sexual behavior, civil rights as defined by the constitution, soldiers must obey military discipline, such as laws in handling prisoners etc.; investors need to conduct business ethically. Individuals differ in conforming to norms; failing individuals feel emotionally disturbed, may experience remorse and social punishments.

Traditional preparations in entering the adult community is learning about rules of conduct in a number of training experiences. The Bar Mitzvah ritual trains youth to be able to read a foreign language, indeed singing it, but also assuming power by assuming a critical position in a related speech. There are no formal trainings for most normative systems. But such training is useful. Psychotherapy services patients; but the well public needs training in wellness as explanations about emotions, about modalities, clarifying the nature of the unconscious as the innate processor of emotions. The public needs to understand the alternative ways of resolving conflicts. Contemporary emotional education has been assumed by organizational training such as mindfulness, a well-accepted spirituality. New progress has been offered by Daniel Goleman's Emotional Intelligence and Ariane Huffington's Thrive. The problem of these training alternatives is that they do not understand the unconscious as a dialectic of emotions and as alternative modalities. This is the focus of 'Creativity and Power Management' a concise program of emotional education.

2.2.2 The emotional education curriculum

My vision is to create awareness of the scientific study of behavior shifting the focus of education from encyclopedic knowledge to learning about the Science of Conflict Resolution and experiencing its applications in the analysis of emotions and of normative systems. It is important to recognize how our emotions affect our perception of reality, and how understanding the distortions of perceptions can improve communications and reduce personal and interpersonal pathology. Education may reduce conflicts and make the world a safe place for all.

Based on the findings of the Moral Science studying the unconscious as a scientific conflict resolving entity through the analysis of the creative process an emotional education program has been developed identified as 'Creativity and Power Management'. It is a well-structured emotional education program founded on the analysis of the creative process as a scientific conflict resolution mechanism. The curriculum is defined as a concise program of science-based emotional education suitable for the classroom, useful for patients as well as for the training of professionals and the general public. The curriculum consists of three segments pursuing the three objectives of the core curriculum of universities: integrating art and science, delivering self-knowledge and clarifying moral values. The integration of art and science is facilitated by viewing the art exhibits of the Museum of the Creative Process. The art exhibits demonstrate the scientific and moral nature of the unconscious. The objective of self-knowledge is attained by examining the personal creativity utilizing the Conflict Analysis Battery. The self-assessment makes a person conscious of the unconscious as an emotional education. It consists of completing creativity tasks reconstructing the syndromal process to identify one's dialectic pattern of emotions, and in completing a personality inventory to identify one's relational alternatives and pathology in terms of intensity of conflicts experience. The third component is the examination of normative systems by studying the evolution of religions as discoveries of the alternative ways of resolving conflict increasing in abstraction of the divine and by improving the resolution of conflicts of the family. We study normative systems in the Moral Monopoly game retracing the evolution of religions as complementary discoveries of conflict resolutions redefining the moral authority of the divine. The study demystifies religions and unites them into the abstract science of the human unconscious. Moral values are identified as the universal scientific principles of conflict resolution. Accordingly, mindfulness is a unifying spirituality approach promoting self-restraint, as reduction of conflict evoking desires. Mindfulness values compassion as the response to reality reducing competitiveness and alienating, antagonistic desire for power.

Science clarifies the science underlying the moral values of mindfulness as moderation, cooperation and mutual respect.

The Moral Science concepts and practices challenge agnostic medicalized psychology and theistic religions by introducing clear parameters in examining psychological and sociological wellness, pathology, and morality. Science challenges both current therapeutic interventions and belief systems. Scientific parameters introduce accountability for both individual and ideological relational choices. The science introduces the abstract analysis of psychological and sociological reality through the examination of the creative process, reflecting the unconscious objectively as having a structure, a six-role process leading to four relational modality choices. We identify accordingly issues of power and attitude that interfere with optimal performance. The emotional education prepares a person by knowing about oneself and about social systems. It prepares a person to navigate life's journey consciously about choices of power and attitude.

2.2.3 Online validation studies

The key educational device in becoming self-aware of one's emotional pattern is in completing the Conflict Analysis Battery, a self-assessment. The process captures the person's syndrome as the correlation of the six-role states as an emotional dialectic simply by completing a set of creativity exercises. The metaphor tests depart from a conflict, stress and end with a compromise. The analysis of the metaphor exercises generates emotions and also insights and recognition of needed changes. The personality inventory (Relational Modality Evaluation Scale, RMES) is diagnostic; it identifies one's modality or spectrum thereof. The two instruments: the inventory and the projectives identify the unconscious as a meaningful emotional cathartic experience.

The completing the self-assessment without any professional services is attested in the statements of 47 individuals who completed the assessment online compensated with the method of Amazon's group of test takers, Mechanical Turk. The statements of these individuals identify the clinical function of the experience in two approaches. One, is examining three areas of emotional growth fulfilling the program's three objectives by using a query of 19 statements. Has the experience been didactic by learning about the new concepts of the unconscious and relational modalities, has it been diagnostic by identifying one's psychodynamic relational pattern, and has it been therapeutic by generating insights and guidance for changes? Another approach to evaluate the experience is by seeking comments from the test takers about the impact of the testing's emotional experience.

Summary of statistics on a group of 47 test takers regarding the assessment experience [13]. The query results confirm the effectiveness of the online delivery of the battery as an emotional education program that is educational, diagnostic and therapeutic.

The query results of the online delivery of the testing yield statistical evidence that we have a didactic, diagnostic and therapeutic instrument. The results attest that the Formal Theoretical hypothesis on the nature of the human unconscious is correct. The Query results validate the formal theoretical conceptualization and the assessment technology. It is important to consider this conceptual and technological approach as providing clarity on behavior as a science and also as generating an effective clinical and therapeutic intervention through an educational delivery.

Participants' query responses, excerpted from [13] are presented as follows:

2.2.4 The program was didactic

The Power Management Program was informative about the concept of the unconscious as a conflict resolving entity. *Agree: 91%.*

The Power Management Program provided clear information about relational modalities as well- ness categories. *Agree: 77%.*

I felt the Power Management Program helped me gain understanding about the nature of the un- conscious as an orderly conflict resolution mechanism. *Agree: 87%*

2.2.5 The program was diagnostic

It helped me to identify my relational pattern. *Agree: 86%*

Identifying my relational pattern helped me to better understand myself. *Agree: 87%*

The Power Management Program helped me understand the conflict resolution process as a sequence of six emotions: stress, response, anxiety, defense, reversal, and compromise. *Agree: 76%*

This program helped me to identify changes to improve my relational adjustment. *Agree: 83%*

I found that the six-role template, combining images and text, integrated fragments of my life into a meaningful conflict resolution pattern. Agree*: 75%*

2.2.6 The program was therapeutic

Completing the creativity component was an emotional experience. *Agree: 83%*

I identified with one or both of the characters in the narrative stories that I created. *Agree: 96%*

This program offered me new information about myself. *Agree: 79%*

I was surprised by the personal relevance of the creativity component. *Agree: 70%*

The creativity component was therapeutic; the metaphors helped me to better understand myself and to also think of making changes. *Agree: 70%*

I was surprised by how much insight I gathered. Agree*: 80%*

This program helped me identify how to better manage power. *Agree: 70%*

After taking this survey, I feel more motivated to make changes in my life. *Agree: 85%*

I think that this survey would be useful for high school students. *Agree: 75%*

I think that this survey would be useful for clinical evaluations. *Agree: 89%*

The program offered me both diagnostic and therapeutic information about myself. *Agree: 83%*

2.2.7 Comments of test takers upon completing the online self-assessment as an emotional experience

While we seek the technical evidence of the process examining the associations generated as a scientific mechanism, the syndrome and the relational modalities, we also examine the clinical benefit of insights generated by the assessment. The test taker experiences clinically emotional relief and insights about one's unconscious pattern through the assessment. S/he identifies one's personality type as a relational modality resolving conflicts, and also identifies changes that can reduce discomfort or maladaptive adjustment (**Table 5**).

Reflecting on the program as a whole, please share your thoughts and feelings about this learning experience.
"*It really makes you look at yourself and assess what's going on in your life.* It was a good experience and I hope I can improve my quality of life by making gradual changes to how I think about things."
"It's been an interesting experience! *I feel like I've learned some new things about myself and had the chance to look at myself in a new way*. I definitely feel emotionally exhausted, so I think my emotions and inner self got a good workout in!"
"*I thought this experience was very unique. I am surprised I was able to learn so much about myself that I didn't realize*. I never knew that events from my past really shaped the life I have now. You don't really see the connections as you are going through them but see the pictures and what I wrote laid out in a sequence was eye-opening."
"It was fun but very strange."
"*This helped get a lot of feeling out.* i learned somethings about myself like I'm not a good drawer, but i digress. This was a fun and interesting way of learning those things. I feel like some weight has been lifted."
"It was hard at times, but *there was a reoccurring theme throughout my life that became more apparent as the study progressed*. I will continue to be kind to myself, and to protect myself from people that are not healthy for me."
"This was very interesting! I did not know what to expect going in, but I actually had a lot of fun participating. I knew a lot of these things already, but some of my drawings really surprised me when I was asked to talk more in depth about them."
"*I really enjoyed it.* I am not very good at the drawing part of it but i enjoyed trying and thinking about the different scenarios."
"I think it was a great program to find out about oneself. It was kind of like digital meditation. I was able to recall and think about past memories and visualize them with the drawings."
Note: Iitalics added for emphasis.

Table 5.
Comments of test takers about the self-assessment experience.

3. Conclusion: the conceptual revamping of psychology into the Moral Science

This essay introduces the formal theoretical conceptualization of the unconscious as the unit order of the social sciences integrating the disciplines of psychology into the Science of Conflict Resolution, abbreviated as the Moral Science. The key premise of the Formal Theory is that emotions are energetic entities and that the unconscious is a conflict resolving energy and attitude transformation mechanism founded on two phenomena of science. Three pendulum oscillations capture energy and three formal operations change a person's attitude, experienced as catharsis. The energized and formalized unconscious accounts for wellness diagnoses as the alternative ways of resolving conflicts, the development of a self-assessment identifying the two components of the unconscious, syndromal structure and relational modalities, and the understanding of religions as complementary discoveries of the sanctified four key conflict resolution alternatives.

The practical significance of the new conceptualization is in its capacity to deliver clinical and educational services illustrated with the application of the new concepts in a self-assessment for the meaningful understanding of oneself. The effectiveness of the self-assessment as a concise program of emotional education is demonstrated in the statistical analysis of responses to a query, and the personal comments on the experience. These testimonials present convincing evidence of the self-assessment's effectiveness as a didactic, diagnostic and therapeutic online intervention providing a meaningful emotional experience without requiring professional services. Self-awareness of the unconscious leads the person to conceive relational modifications optimizing relational choices. This sample delivery of the assessment is relevant for the delivery of a more extensive program of emotional education to the general public and for the delivery of the program for therapeutic services.

The effectiveness of the assessment experience validates the formal theoretical premise on the nature of the unconscious as the unit of the social sciences. The entity is shown to be a measurable natural science, conflict resolving phenomenon that leads to wellness diagnostic categories, the four relational modalities.

The conclusion from this essay and the brief sample of its validation is that the formal conceptual position challenges current diagnostic, therapeutic, educational and religious concepts and practices by introducing a promising alternative paradigm, identifying the unconscious rigorous conceptualization founded on the study of the creative process. We may conclude that this conceptual innovation challenges current psychological theory and practices [14], and that it demystifies religions as biased dogma based psychological theories. The formal theoretical conceptualization introduces a quantum leap in the social sciences by reconciling psychology and morality, art and science, biology and sociology, and integrating religions into the Science of Conflict Resolution, the Moral Science.

4. Limitations

This model's impact may be constrained by individuals' cognitive ability, willingness to engage in training program, and emotional readiness to experiment with self-examination. Accessing the online program, requires some technical skills and internet availability.

Author details

Albert Levis
Museum of the Creative Process, Manchester, VT, USA

*Address all correspondence to: moralscience@hotmail.com

References

[1] Levis A, Levis M. The Moral Science Primer: Psychology As the Science of Conflict Resolution. Manchester, VT: Normative Publications; 2023

[2] Levis AJ. Conflict Analysis: The Formal Theory of Behavior: A Theory and its Experimental Validation. Manchester, VT: Normative Publications; 1988

[3] Royce J. Royce's Logical Essays: Collected Logical Essays of Josiah Royce. Dubuque, IA: W.C. Brown Co; 1951

[4] Levis AJ, Levis M. Science Stealing the Fire of the Gods and Healing the World. 1st ed. Manchester, VT: Normative Publications; 2011

[5] Levis AJ, Levis M. Creativity and Power Management: A Concise Program of Emotional Education. Vol. 1. Manchester, VT: Normative Publications; 2015

[6] Levis AJ. Artificial Intelligence Confirming the Formal Theoretical Premise. Museum of the Creative Process; 2023. Available from: https://www.museumofthecreativeprocess.com/workshop

[7] Levis AJ. The formal theory of behaviour. The International Journal of Social Psychiatry. 1977;**23**(2):79-93

[8] Aristotle. Aristotle's Poetics (S. Halliwell, Trans.). Chicago, IL: University of Chicago Press; 1998

[9] American Psychiatric Association. Diagnostic and Statistical Manual of Mental Disorders: DSM-5. 5th ed. Washington DC: American Psychiatric Association; 2013

[10] Levis AJ. Conflict Analysis Training: A Program of Emotional Education. Manchester, VT: Normative Publications; 1988

[11] Levis A, Levis M. A therapy outcome case study applying formal theory's concepts: Revamping psychology into the science of conflict resolution, The Moral Science [Preprint], PsyArXiv. 2019. DOI: 10.31234/osf.io/kq4jn

[12] Levis AJ. Shifting our attention from content to process. Journal of Psychotherapy Integration. 1996;**6**(2):127-134. DOI: 10.1037/h0101107

[13] Levis AJ, Levis M. Creativity and Power Management: A Concise Program of Emotional Education. Vol. 2. Manchester, VT: Normative Publications; 2015

[14] Sharpless BA, Barber JP. Schools of Psychotherapy and the Beginnings of a Scientific Approach. Oxford, UK: Oxford Handbook; 2010

Chapter 2

Ethical Considerations in Organizational Conflict

Josh Hyatt and Jeffrey Gruenglas

Abstract

Ethical considerations are critical to decision-making in any organization. Decisions that impact internal and external stakeholders carry implications that account for employee conduct, personal values, institutional policies, and obligations to customers. Conflicts within an organization present a particularly unique set of dynamics and tensions that require ethical assessment to ensure a fair, equitable, and ethically acceptable work environment. Recognizing these ethical challenges, and ultimately addressing and resolving them, is incumbent upon all stakeholders to ensure the success of the organization and its stated mission to employees, clients, and the community it serves. This chapter explores commonly encountered forms of organizational conflicts with respect to ethical concerns, and the considerations for navigating such conditions through theoretical foundations and a practical lens. The discussion is then followed by a framework for advancing ethical conduct through institutional codes and policies. We conclude with a case study that examines the ethical challenge of fair resource allocation and just distribution of goods.

Keywords: ethics, morals, values, organizational conflict, conflict of interest

1. Introduction

How does one successfully approach organizational challenges in a fair and just manner? This question remains a moral and political concern of every manager who has had to ponder, "what is the right thing to do?" The question takes an even more complex turn when multiple stakeholders are involved in the decision. Consider a simple job promotion. Is the promotion of one employee fair to other employees who may be equally deserving of the same recognition? How does this decision affect the manager's obligation to the organization and its fiduciary responsibility to cost-saving-minded investors? To what extent is the manager unduly influenced by an existing relationship with the rewarded employee? These questions only the scratch the very surface of ethically appropriate decisions and beckon any organization to examine relationships among stakeholders, corporate values, and personal morals that make ethical decision-making complex and worthy of careful deliberation.

In the current climate of constant organizational change, ethical decisions are fundamental to the challenge that each of us face daily both in our personal and professional lives. Change in organizations is inevitable but also embodies complexities of navigating ethical and moral boundaries. Ethical conflicts in the workplace have profound effects on morals, code of conduct, and norms among stakeholders, which can ultimately undermine an organizational mission and its articulated values.

There is no one-size-fits-all approach to arriving at the ideal ethical resolution to every problem, and this contributes to the daunting task of exacting decisions that at best are fair and minimize harm to others. Knowing how to navigate situations as they arise within the organization is vital to the health and wellbeing of the company; but it is equally important to know and understand how the change and ethical practices will impact the stakeholders involved. In a professional setting it is our collective responsibility to understand what is needed to invoke positive change within an organization, and in turn making an impact for the greater good.

This chapter explores ethical considerations within organizations and defines the ethical challenges and their manifestation in the general work environment. We present various accepted ethical models and paradigms for addressing such challenges and propose practical approaches for addressing these barriers. We further describe theories and moral concepts to help effectively navigate change processes and ethical dilemmas and conclude by presenting and unpacking a real-world case study within industry to challenge the reader with how ethical challenges manifest and are addressed through a systematic process.

2. Manifestations of ethical conflict

Organizational change often introduces uncertainties and ambiguities, which can breed conflicts. When employees face uncertainty about their future, roles, or the impact of changes on their job security, conflicts can arise from fear, resistance, or frustration. Power struggles may surface as individuals vie for influence or attempt to safeguard their positions amidst the shifting organizational landscape. Furthermore, conflicts can stem from conflicting priorities that emerge during organizational change [1]. Different stakeholders may have varying interests and visions for the organization, leading to disagreements and conflicts over resource allocation, decision-making authority, or the overall direction the organization should take.

Organizational change can be met with resistance to change, particularly when stakeholders have a narrow interest, misunderstanding and lack of trust, apply different evaluations, and have a low tolerance for change itself. It is critical for any decision-maker to recognize that such variances may manifest as conflict but also reflect on the possibility that competing interests can be equally valid and compelling with respect to the employee. Such interests can be guided by indirect profit, gain, collective benefits, or the benefits for the individual—all of which may be valid and real. Likewise, the inevitability of conflict can be a product of differing attitudes, beliefs, levels of knowledge, and life experiences. Not surprisingly, opposing values often lead to self-centeredness and barriers to understanding other perspectives, and in more severe forms, protectionism and self-preservation [2].

2.1 Organizational conflict

Conflict is a natural consequence of communication, and organizational conflict is an inherent aspect of any complex system. It arises due to the diverse nature of individuals, their varied perspectives, interests, goals, and complex interactions between different parts of the organization. Conflicts are not inherently harmful or destructive; they can serve as catalysts for growth, innovation, and positive change when managed effectively by bringing different viewpoints to the table, challenging existing assumptions, and fostering creative problem-solving. Conflicts in organizations often stem from differences in values, priorities, or resources. As individuals work together towards common goals, their perspectives may clash, resulting in tensions or disagreements. These conflicts can occur at various organizational levels, including individuals, teams, departments, or even between organizational units [3].

2.1.1 Types of organizational conflicts

The types of conflicts are varied and often circumstantial and described into two principal categories: personal and systemic. Personal conflicts include interpersonal conflicts, conflicts of interest, and ethical conflicts. Systemic conflicts include role, structural, cultural, and conflict between strategy and execution [4]. The following describe various ways in which such conflict modalities can present:

- Interpersonal conflicts occur between individuals or groups within the organization and are driven by differences in personalities, communication styles, or personal values. They may arise due to misunderstandings, conflicting goals, power struggles, or competition for resources or recognition.

- Conflicts of interest occur when individuals or groups have competing personal or professional interests that may compromise their ability to act objectively and, in the organization's, best interest. Examples include situations where personal relationships, financial gain, or external affiliations influence decision-making. Ethical conflicts arise when disagreements or dilemmas are related to ethical principles, values, or behaviors within the organization. These conflicts may occur when there are competing ethical standards, differing interpretations of ethical guidelines, or conflicts between personal and organizational ethics.

- Organizational conflict and ethical decision-making are closely linked because conflicts often involve ethical dilemmas requiring thoughtful consideration and analysis.

- Role conflicts emerge when individuals or groups have conflicting expectations or demands placed upon them. These conflicts can arise from unclear job responsibilities, overlapping roles, conflicting priorities, or organizational or departmental goals differences.

- Structural conflicts stem from organizational structures, processes, or systems. These conflicts often arise when there are conflicting goals or interests between different departments, units, or hierarchical levels within the organization. Inadequate communication channels, lack of coordination, or resource allocation issues can contribute to structural conflicts.

- Cultural conflicts emerge when there are differences in values, norms, beliefs, or expectations among individuals or groups within the organization. These conflicts may arise due to diversity, such as different ethnic or cultural backgrounds, or from clashes between subcultures within the organization.

- Conflicts between strategy and execution occur when there is a disconnect between the strategic goals or objectives of the organization and the ability to implement or execute those strategies effectively. Misalignment between strategic decisions and operational realities can lead to conflicts and inefficiencies.

2.1.2 Reasons for organizational conflict

The reasons for these conflicts can vary widely depending on the specific circumstances and dynamics of the organization. Poor communication, inadequate leadership, limited resources, conflicting goals, organizational change, and lack of clarity or alignment in roles and responsibilities can contribute to organizational conflicts. Yet primary reasons for organizational conflict include communication, complexity, and culture. These arise from multiple contributing factors:

- **Communication.** Organizational conflict often arises due to a communication breakdown attributed to several factors. Poor communication channels, characterized by ineffective or insufficient means of information exchange, play a significant role in fostering conflicts within an organization. When the channels fail to facilitate clear and timely communication, this creates an environment where misunderstandings and misinterpretations of messages can occur.

- **Misinterpretation of messages further compounds the problem.** Individuals may perceive and understand information differently based on their filters, biases, and interpretations. Nonverbal cues, such as body language or tone of voice, can be easily misread or misinterpreted, adding complexity to the communication process. Cultural and language differences can also contribute to misinterpretations, as people may ascribe different meanings to words or expressions.

- **Lack of clarity in communication.** Unclear messages, vague instructions, or undefined roles and responsibilities can create employee confusion and uncertainty. When individuals are unsure about what is expected of them or have conflicting perceptions of their roles, this increases the likelihood of misunderstandings and disagreements that can in turn escalate into conflict.

- **Power dynamics.** Power imbalances stemming from hierarchical structures, formal authority, or informal influence can create tensions and fuel conflicts. Individuals who feel marginalized, unheard, or unfairly treated may resist or challenge authority, leading to strained relationships and communication breakdowns. Power struggles and competition for dominance can impede effective communication, as individuals may hesitate to express their opinions or concerns openly.

- **Competition for limited resources.** When resources such as funding, staffing, or time are scarce, individuals or teams may vie for their fair share, leading to heightened tensions and conflicts. Communication breakdowns related to resource allocation decisions or perceived inequities in distribution can intensify these conflicts.

- **Varying levels of authority.** Conflicts can arise when decision-making processes need more transparency and clarity in roles and responsibilities. Individuals may feel excluded from decision-making processes, perceive favoritism, or resist top-down directives, resulting in communication gaps and disagreements.

Diverse groups often consist of individuals with contrasting perspectives, beliefs, and ways of approaching tasks. Varying work styles, such as those who prefer structure and adherence to processes versus those who thrive in a more flexible and innovative environment, can lead to conflicts over preferred methods and approaches. Differences in personalities, such as introverts versus extroverts or risk-averse versus risk-takers, can further exacerbate conflicts as contrasting working styles and communication preferences come into play. Moreover, conflicts can emerge during times of organizational change. Restructuring efforts, mergers, or shifts in strategic direction inherently disrupt established norms, power dynamics, and relationships within the organization. Changes in reporting lines, team composition, or job roles can trigger conflicts as individuals adjust to new responsibilities or perceive a threat to their status or authority. Conflicts may also arise when individuals resist or struggle to adapt to the changes, leading to clashes between those embracing and resisting the change.

Addressing these contributing factors requires organizations to prioritize effective communication. Approaches include improving communication channels, promoting clarity in messaging, encouraging active listening, and addressing power imbalances. Organizations can also foster a culture of collaboration, teamwork, and shared goals to minimize conflicts stemming from competition for resources or discrepancies in authority. Organizations can mitigate conflicts and create a more harmonious work environment by recognizing the impact of communication breakdown and proactively working to enhance communication processes. Encouraging open dialog, fostering an inclusive culture that respects diverse perspectives, providing support and resources during change, and promoting collaboration can help mitigate conflicts. Leaders play a crucial role in managing conflicts by facilitating discussions, mediating disputes, and promoting a shared vision that unifies individuals and aligns their efforts towards organizational goals.

3. Navigating ethical conflict

The ethical approach to addressing organizational conflict may be as varied as the complexity of the situation itself. The multiple perspectives allow professionals to leverage a toolkit from which to apply a systematic approach to ethical decision-making. Any change in an organization brings about concerns of inequities, fairness, and conflict of interest. Coupled with perceptions of the influence of power dynamics and personal agenda, it is not surprising that organizations and their managers struggle to operate under an ethical code of conduct. Such decisions may be driven by factors across multiple levels. These include developmental, to improve on a singular approach, process, or project; transitional, to allow organizations to shift or evolve towards new processes or goals; and transformational, a complete rethinking of an organization's vision, culture, behavior, dynamic, business model, management approach, or personnel.

3.1 Multiple theories, multiple permutations

Designing an ethical organization is hard work but a worthwhile and often necessary endeavor. Ethics are not just a belief problem but a design problem. Given the range of stakeholder values, thoughts with judgment, incentives, and cultural norms, organizations must act on principles that satisfy core tenets that align with stakeholder values. All moral theories from which ethical applications are derived can be positioned between two opposing yet non-mutually exclusive tenets: the obligation of one's duty and the act of promoting happiness as a consequence. These moral perspectives, philosophically termed Deontology and Consequentialism, respectively, each carry a unique set of characteristics for how we act as individuals and with one another. Generally described, the Deontological reasoning asserts that a theory of duty holding that some features of actions other than or in addition to consequences make actions right or wrong, whereas a utilitarian model advocates for actions are right or wrong according to the balance of their good and bad consequences.

3.1.1 Ethics and values-based decision making

Within a professional atmosphere, broad-stroke fundamental theories are rarely sufficient to guide ethical considerations in complex decisions that affect employees with varying values, cultural leanings, religious and ideological affiliations, and personal morals. In this context, rather, one needs to extend beyond normative ethics and consider an additional layer of ethical attributes that help guide the complex dynamics of organizational hierarchy and interpersonal dynamics. These include stewardship, loyalty, and fidelity. Finally, we examine the concept and application of principlism, an ethical approach to decision-making that embodies a set of principles and standards that can be universally applied to moral challenges with the workplace.

Values are not necessarily universal; they reflect the relative morals and personal codes that individuals assign to their conduct in society. They are also embedded in political and societal cultures. Social norms are principles or guidelines that guide action and decisions. These may present tension with normative practices (conventions, customs and ideals). Moral authority and relativism embody emotion and experiential factors that may contribute to one's normative approach to ethics. Cultural values and international differences may also contribute to a social and cultural environment governed by laws, rules and regulations, formal values and norms, codes of conduct, and policies.

3.1.2 Integrating morals and values

When we discuss morality and values, what does this mean in a practical sense? The terms are "loaded," meaning they mean different things to different people. Some may see morals as personal beliefs shaped by upbringing and experience, and values are what shape our actions and behaviors. Though morals and values are fundamental concepts in ethics and play a significant role in shaping an individuals' beliefs, attitudes, and behavior, they are different yet closely related.

Morals are principles or standards of conduct, deeply ingrained from cultural, social, religious, and personal factors, that guide individuals in distinguishing right from wrong. Morals typically encompass ethical principles and judgments about what is morally good or bad, right or wrong, virtuous or vicious. They serve as a foundation for ethical decision-making and provide a framework for individuals to navigate their actions and interactions with others.

From this foundational perspective comes moral theory, a vast range of philosophical frameworks that aim to understand ethics and guide human behavior systematically. Moral theory encompasses two fundamental components: the theory of right conduct (provide guidelines for determining what actions are morally right or wrong by exploring the concepts of moral obligations and duties) and the theory of value (most traditionally accepted that the value of any object or service is transient and correlated by the work input and cost of resources). By examining these moral foundations, principles, and practical implications, we can gain a deeper understanding of the complexities involved in ethical decision-making.

Whereas morals focus more on distinguishing right from wrong, values are broader and encompass a more comprehensive range of beliefs and ideals that individuals consider significant in shaping their lives and decision-making. Morals are often derived from, and aligned with, one's values, but they specifically address ethical conduct and decision-making. Values are individuals' fundamental beliefs or ideals, which influence their attitudes, choices, and behaviors. They assist in prioritizing and making choices that align with their core beliefs and principles. They reflect what individuals consider important, desirable, or worthwhile in life. Values encompass various domains such as personal, social, professional, or spiritual aspects and often include principles like honesty, integrity, respect, compassion, fairness, loyalty, freedom, equality, and justice.

Illustration: Consider the principle of honesty. Honesty is a moral virtue that involves telling the truth, being sincere, and avoiding deceit. It is morally right to be honest and morally wrong to lie or deceive others, and this frame guides individuals in situations where truthfulness is expected or necessary. However, the application is based on the context of the situation. Is it ever morally justified not to be entirely truthful or transparent? Consider the value of compassion. Compassion is a virtue that many individuals hold dear. It involves showing empathy, kindness, and concern for the well-being of others. People who value compassion strive to alleviate suffering, help those in need, and promote understanding and support in their relationships and communities. Compassion influences individuals' choices, such as volunteering for charitable causes or assisting those facing hardships. In this example, honesty represents a moral principle that guides ethical conduct, distinguishing between truthful and deceptive behavior. Conversely, compassion represents a broader value reflecting a deep-seated belief in empathy and kindness towards others that encompasses honesty.

Now consider an example where a moral principle builds on a core value. We would explore respecting others, which is a key component of corporate diversity, equity, and inclusion programming. The moral foundation for this topic is non-discrimination, which dictates that individuals should not be treated unfairly or prejudiced based on characteristics such as race, gender, religion, sexual orientation, or any other inherent or acquired trait. Non-discrimination upholds the belief that everyone deserves equal treatment and opportunities, irrespective of their differences. This moral foundation can lead us to respect others, a core value that emphasizes treating individuals with dignity, acknowledging their worth, and recognizing their rights and autonomy. It also involves showing consideration, listening attentively, valuing diverse perspectives, and accepting that not everyone starts at the same starting line. In this example, the moral principle of non-discrimination provides the foundation for the value of respecting others and providing supportive conditions to address inequities faced by marginalized or vulnerable populations. Conversely, by valuing and respecting one's inherent worth and dignity, the moral principle of non-discrimination extends that respect further by advocating for just treatment and opposing unfair biases or prejudices.

3.1.3 Moral injury and conflict

Morals and values vary among individuals, cultures, and societies. They are also subject to interpretation and context; what is considered morally acceptable or valuable in one situation may differ in another. Additionally, individuals may prioritize and interpret morals and values differently based on their experiences, upbringing, and cultural background.

What happens when we act contrary to our morals and values? Moral conflicts occur when individuals or groups make decisions or take actions that involve conflicting ethical principles or values. These conflicts arise when two or more moral principles or values conflict, making the determination of the right course of action challenging. As with morals and values, moral conflicts are contextual, such as personal dilemmas, professional settings, societal issues, or political determinates. Moral conflicts often challenge individuals to weigh the importance of competing moral principles, evaluate the potential consequences of their choices, and make decisions that align with their values or ethical frameworks. Resolving moral conflicts requires thoughtful consideration, ethical reasoning, and a willingness to engage in dialog to find a balance or compromise that minimizes harm and upholds ethical standards. Several examples briefly highlight such moral conflicts. Consider how you may choose to act in each case:

1. **Honesty vs. loyalty:** Imagine a situation where a person discovers that a close friend has committed a serious offense. They face a moral conflict between being honest about their friend's actions, which may result in severe consequences, or remaining loyal and protecting their friend from potential harm.

2. **Autonomy vs. paternalism:** In healthcare there may be a conflict between respecting a patient's autonomy (their right to make decisions about their healthcare) and acting in their best interest. For example, a doctor might recommend a specific treatment they believe is best for the patient's health, but the patient refuses it based on their beliefs or values.

3. **Utilitarianism vs. individual rights:** The ethical theory of utilitarianism promotes maximizing overall happiness or well-being for the greatest number of people. However, conflicts can arise when the pursuing of the greater good clashes with individual rights or freedoms. For instance, a government might implement a policy restricting certain civil liberties for public safety, leading to a conflict between promoting the common good and respecting individual rights.

4. **Environmental preservation vs. economic development:** This conflict arises when decisions regarding using natural resources or land clash with the moral value of preserving the environment for future generations or the economic interests or immediate benefits of exploiting those resources for development or profit.

3.1.4 Implicit bias and prejudice

Implicit bias and moral injury are two distinct concepts that relate to different aspects of human behavior and experience. Implicit bias refers to the unconscious attitudes and stereotypes that individuals hold towards certain groups of people, which can influence their judgments and actions [5]. These biases are often formed through socialization and cultural factors and may contradict an individual's explicit beliefs or values. Implicit biases can manifest in various domains, such as race, gender, age, or socioeconomic status, affect decision-making processes, and contribute to systemic inequalities and discrimination. While implicit bias and moral injury are separate concepts, some connections may exist between them in specific contexts. For example, individuals who hold implicit biases against certain groups may experience moral injury if their biased attitudes lead them to act in ways that contradict their explicit moral values. Being the target of implicit bias can contribute to moral injury if individuals feel devalued or morally violated by the discriminatory treatment they receive.

It is essential to address both implicit bias and moral injury to promote fairness, justice, and well-being. Strategies such as awareness training, education, and creating inclusive environments can help mitigate the effects of implicit bias. Addressing moral injury requires support and interventions that foster healing, moral resilience, and restoring a sense of meaning and purpose in individuals who have experienced moral harm and/or conflict.

3.1.5 Risk-taking behaviors

Risk-taking behaviors are a typical response to coping with or mitigating moral injury's effects. These behaviors can take various forms and span a wide range of actions. People may engage in substance abuse, self-destructive behaviors, impulsive decision-making, aggression, thrill-seeking activities, or even isolate themselves to deal with the distressing emotions associated with moral injury. These behaviors serve as maladaptive coping mechanisms that temporarily escape the overwhelming feelings. Risk-taking or impulsive actions allow individuals to regain a sense of control or reclaim lost identity and meaning.

When staff members exhibit risk-taking behaviors within an organizational context, it can have significant impact. The consequences may vary depending on the nature and severity of the behaviors and the specific industry and circumstances involved. It may have legal and compliance concerns, such as involving illegal activities or violations of company policies that can expose the organization to legal and compliance risks. This may trigger legal recourse, regulatory penalties, damage to the company's reputation, and potential loss of business opportunities. Decreased productivity and performance are noted when staff members engage in risk-taking behaviors; their focus may shift away from work responsibilities, resulting in decreased productivity, missed deadlines, poor decision-making, and overall reduced performance. It can also affect team dynamics and collaboration. Employee morale and retention may further suffer when staff members engage in behaviors that can negatively impact overall employee morale and job satisfaction. Co-workers may feel demoralized, lose trust in their colleagues, or perceive a lack of fairness within the organization, contributing to increased turnover and difficulties attracting and retaining talented employees.

3.1.6 Culture impact and psychological safety

Organizations and communities are vital to fostering ethical cultures promoting accountability and integrity. By implementing ethical codes that outline expected conduct, providing moral education and training to employees, and establishing mechanisms for ethical decision-making and oversight, organizations can create an environment that minimizes moral disengagement and encourages individuals to uphold their moral values.

Building a culture of psychological safety is essential in this context. When individuals feel safe to voice their concerns, ask questions, and express their moral perspectives without fear of reprisal or judgment, it facilitates open dialog and constructive discussions about ethical dilemmas. Psychological safety nurtures trust and respect, allowing individuals to openly reflect on their experiences and engage in collaborative problem-solving to address moral challenges. Furthermore, organizations can support employees in their moral growth by offering resources for moral development, such as workshops, mentoring programs, or opportunities for shared moral reflection. By actively investing in the ethical development of their workforce, organizations demonstrate a commitment to fostering an ethical culture that prioritizes moral decision-making and integrity.

The cultural impact of promoting ethical decision-making extends beyond the organization itself. Communities can also nurture an ethical environment by encouraging dialog and reflection on moral issues and creating spaces for shared understanding and growth. Collaborative efforts involving organizations, educational institutions, and community leaders can promote ethical behavior and moral development on a broader scale. By embracing the importance of psychological safety, actively supporting individuals in their moral growth, and fostering ethical cultures at both the organizational and community levels, society can create an environment that encourages principled decision-making, accountability, and integrity in the face of moral challenges.

The impact of moral injury on moral decision-making is not static. While moral injury can initially disrupt decision-making processes, individuals can heal and grow from moral injuries over time. Seeking support, engaging in moral reflection, and actively working towards personal growth and repair can restore individuals' confidence in their moral judgment and enhance their ability to make principled decisions. At the systemic level, organizations and communities can foster ethical cultures that promote accountability and integrity. Implementing ethical codes, providing moral education and training, and establishing ethical decision-making and oversight mechanisms can help prevent moral disengagement and encourage individuals to uphold their moral values.

4. Advancing adherence to ethical codes

An organization has an ethical duty to its employees and stakeholders to develop and maintain a clear vision and communication plan regarding adherence to ethical codes. These two areas are where intentions and execution can misalign. As we discussed in previous sections, organizations are complex and depend on the individual contributions of their employees. However, a company's biggest asset is its most significant liability, the individual employee. It is imperative that an organization clearly define its vision and ethical expectations and then ensure that its employees align their actions accordingly, which is easier said than done [6, 7].

- **Vision.** A well-defined vision sets the tone for ethical behavior by articulating the organization's goals, purpose, and values. It also serves as a powerful tool for setting the tone of ethical behavior within an organization by providing a framework for decision-making that aligns with its ethical standards. A clear vision ensures that all stakeholders, including employees, understand ethical expectations and work towards achieving common goals. The vision statement encapsulates the long-term aspirations and direction of the organization. It communicates the desired impact the organization aims to achieve and the values that underpin its actions. When explicitly stated in the vision, these values become a guiding light for ethical behavior. Employees and stakeholders can refer to the vision to understand the organization's overarching objectives and the ethical principles governing their actions. It provides a common language and a reference point for discussions and decision-making about ethical dilemmas. When employees have a clear vision to guide them, they can make choices consistent with the organization's values, even in complex situations where ethical dilemmas may arise.

- **Communication plan.** Effective communication is not just a beneficial aspect of organizational functioning but a cornerstone supporting transparency, trust, and accountability within the organization. Through effective communication, ethical concerns and guidelines can be clearly and consistently communicated to all employees and stakeholders. Disseminating ethical codes and standards is crucial in fostering an organizational culture. A communication plan provides a roadmap for sharing these codes and standards with employees at various levels and departments. By establishing a communication plan that outlines channels, protocols, and expectations, the organization can ensure that ethical concerns and guidelines are effectively communicated and understood by everyone involved. It would include disseminating the ethical codes and standards throughout the organization to ensure employees are aware of its values, principles, and guidelines that govern their behavior. This clarity reduces the likelihood of misunderstandings, misinterpretations, or ethical lapses due to ignorance. By establishing open lines of communication, organizations can foster an environment where employees feel comfortable expressing concerns and seeking guidance regarding ethical dilemmas. Transparent communication practices ensure that information about ethical issues, decisions, and processes is shared openly with employees and stakeholders. When employees access relevant information, they can make more informed ethical choices and understand the broader context of their actions.

- **Accountability.** A communication plan sets clear expectations and protocols for reporting ethical violations and breaches. It establishes mechanisms to hold individuals accountable for their actions and ensures that the consequences of unethical behavior are communicated effectively. By doing so, organizations demonstrate their commitment to upholding ethical standards and show that unethical behavior is unacceptable. Transparency and accountability are also enhanced through effective communication, as it ensures that relevant information is shared, and individuals are held responsible for their actions. Ultimately, a culture of ethical behavior is nurtured when communication practices prioritize transparency, trust, and accountability.

- **Mitigating conflicts of interest.** An organization has a fundamental obligation to address conflicts of interest to uphold its integrity and maintain the trust of its stakeholders. Conflicts of interest occur when an individual's interests or obligations interfere with their ability to act in the organization's best interests. By addressing conflicts of interest proactively and transparently, organizations can mitigate the risks associated with such conflicts and ensure fair and ethical decision-making processes.

Illustration: GreenTech Solutions is a fictional company that specializes in renewable energy solutions. GreenTech Solutions understands the importance of ethical conduct in the industry and strives to ensure adherence to ethical codes within the organization. They have a clear vision that outlines their ethical practices and expectations: "To become a leader in sustainable energy solutions while maintaining the highest ethical standards for our clients, employees, and the environment." Their vision statement emphasizes their commitment to environmental stewardship, integrity, and social responsibility. This vision serves as a guiding principle for decision-making processes and ensures that all employees understand the organization's expectations regarding ethical conduct.

From this, GreenTech Solutions develops a communication plan emphasizing transparency and accountability. They regularly conduct training sessions and workshops to educate employees about their ethical standards and the industry's best practices. They provide channels for employees to voice concerns, ask questions, and report any ethical violations they may witness. This open communication fosters a culture of trust and encourages employees to act ethically and responsibly.

If a GreenTech Solutions employee now encounters a potential conflict of interest while working on a project, a clear vision and communication plan help the employee's actions; he or she knows that their decisions should prioritize the company's and its stakeholders' best interests rather than personal gain. They also know they can reach out to the designated channels, such as an ethics hotline or their immediate supervisor, to seek guidance and report the situation.

By having a clear communication plan and vision GreenTech Solutions maintains adherence to ethical codes within the organization and upholds its reputation in the industry. Their commitment to open communication and ethical behavior enhances their credibility among customers, investors, and other stakeholders who value sustainability and responsible business practices.

- **Policies and guidelines.** Establishing clear policies and guidelines regarding conflicts of interest is critical for an organization to address and manage such conflicts effectively. These policies serve as a roadmap that outlines the organization's expectations and procedures for identifying, disclosing, and resolving conflicts of interest. Clearly communicating these policies to employees establishes a foundation for addressing conflicts systematically and fairly. The effective communication of these policies and guidelines is crucial. To achieve this, an organization should consider training programs, regular communication channels, and integrating the policies into the organization's code of conduct or employee handbook. By providing specific examples and scenarios, employees better understand what circumstances might give rise to conflicts of interest.

- **Transparency and disclosure.** Organizations must promote and require transparency and disclosure. Employees should be encouraged and required to disclose any actual or potential conflicts of interest, including financial interests, personal relationships, or other external affiliations that could compromise their objectivity or impartiality. Organizations can effectively identify and manage conflicts of interest by creating an environment where disclosure is valued and protected. When conflicts of interest are identified, organizations have a duty to assess and manage them appropriately. For example, employees with a conflict are asked to recuse themselves from this decision-making process.

- **Education.** Proactive and ongoing education programs about conflicts of interest and their potential consequences are critical. Training programs and workshops can raise awareness about the ethical implications of conflicts and guide how to identify and manage them effectively. Fostering a culture of ethical awareness empowers employees to make informed decisions and act in the organization's best interests.

- **Fairness and equity.** These critical concepts pertain to treating individuals justly and ensuring equal opportunities, access, and treatment for all organization members. Organizations prioritizing fairness and equity create an ethical environment that promotes inclusivity, diversity, and respect. Fairness refers to the fair and unbiased treatment of individuals within an organization. It entails making decisions and allocating resources free from favoritism, discrimination, or bias. Fairness ensures that individuals are treated equitably based on objective criteria and relevant qualifications. This principle extends to various aspects of organizational life, such as hiring and promotion processes, compensation and benefits, performance evaluations, and disciplinary actions. Conversely, equity focuses on ensuring that individuals have equal access to opportunities, resources, and benefits. It recognizes that individuals may have diverse needs, circumstances, and backgrounds. Moreover, fairness and equity align with legal and ethical standards. Organizations are responsible for complying with laws and regulations that promote equal employment opportunities and prevent discrimination. Ethically, fairness and equity reflect principles of justice, human rights, and social responsibility. By incorporating fairness and equity into their ethical framework, organizations demonstrate their commitment to upholding these principles and contributing to a just and inclusive society.

- **Psychological safety.** Fostering an environment of psychological safety is closely intertwined with organizational ethics. Psychological safety exists in an environment where individuals feel safe to express their opinions, ideas, and concerns and can take interpersonal risks without fear of retaliation or punishment. Nurturing psychological safety can significantly contribute to upholding ethical principles and practices because employees feel empowered to raise questions, share their perspectives, and challenge unethical practices without fear of judgment. Conversely, an environment that allows for psychological fear is likely to see an increase in stress, anxiety, and fear levels in the workplace.

Illustration: HealthFirst Hospital recognizes the importance of addressing conflicts of interest to maintain the trust and integrity of its healthcare services. The organization has a clear policy outlining what constitutes a conflict of interest and providing guidelines on managing such situations. The Compliance Officer knows Dr. Smith, a highly regarded specialist at HealthFirst Hospital, has a financial interest in a pharmaceutical company that manufactures a specific medication. The hospital's policy requires all healthcare professionals to disclose any financial interests that may present a conflict of interest.

Upon learning about Dr. Smith's financial interest, the Compliance Officer initiates a process to examine the potential conflict, establishing an independent review committee comprising members with no financial ties to the pharmaceutical company to evaluate the situation objectively. The committee carefully examines the conflict, considering factors such as the potential impact on patient care, the available alternatives, and the extent of Dr. Smith's financial interest. Based on the committee's assessment, it is determined that there is a potential conflict of interest that could compromise impartial decision-making.

The Compliance Officer discusses the conflict with Dr. Smith and requests that he either recuse himself from any decision-making processes involving the prescription and promotion of the medication or that patients are made aware of the conflict and its extent if he plans to prescribe it. These options ensure that patient care remains the top priority and is not influenced by personal financial considerations.

5. Conclusion

Establishing a culture that promotes ethical decision-making is another crucial aspect of managing conflicts effectively. Organizations must provide employees with the necessary tools, resources, and training to navigate ethical dilemmas. This includes developing and disseminating a comprehensive code of conduct, establishing clear policies and procedures, and fostering a supportive environment encouraging ethical behavior and open discussions about moral challenges and dilemmas. Furthermore, creating environments that prioritize ethical conduct, open dialog, and supportive structures can restore moral decision-making capacities. Organizations and communities can foster a culture that encourages reflection, provides opportunities for moral development, and offers spaces for individuals to discuss and process their moral struggles. Such environments are bound to support individuals in rebuilding their moral decision-making capabilities and mitigate the risk of future moral injury. By actively nurturing a culture that promotes psychological safety, values diverse perspectives, encourages ethical behavior, and provides the necessary support structures, organizations create an environment where conflicts are approached constructively. This culture facilitates open dialog, collaborative problem-solving, and the resolution of conflicts in a manner that upholds the well-being of individuals and the organization as a whole.

While conflict in the workplace cannot be eliminated entirely, organizations can adopt strategies to manage and resolve them effectively. Encouraging open and honest communication, active listening, and respectful dialog can facilitate understanding and empathy among conflicting parties. Conflict resolution techniques such as negotiation, mediation, and compromise can help find mutually acceptable solutions. It is essential for organizations to proactively address these underlying factors and implement effective conflict management strategies to minimize the negative impact of conflicts and foster a healthy and productive work environment.

Morals and values serve as guiding principles that shape individual and organizational ethical perspectives, influence their behavior, and contribute to the formation of integrity that is rooted in the mission, vision, and perception of stakeholders. Practically they provide a framework for individuals and organizations to evaluate actions, make moral judgments, and strive for a meaningful and virtuous impact on one another and society as a whole.

6. Case study: "Who gets the vaccine?"

The following case study presents a real-world illustration of an organizational issue surrounding fair and equitable distribution of services within a public health context. Although identifiers have been removed, the specifics reflect realistic ethical challenges and considerations when resolving complex ethical conflict within an organization.

Situation and background

A 22-year-old college student named Maria with a compromised immune system is at risk of respiratory infections, for which she has been periodically hospitalized since she was a child. The student is a candidate to receive a vaccine to protect against an emerging virus, which can mitigate her risk of contracting the virus, leading to health complications, hospitalization, and even death.

Nationwide shortages have resulted in the vaccine available in limited quantities, forcing clinics and health care providers to make the difficult decision of allocating the available resources to the populations in greatest need. To complicate matters, the decision is at the discretion of the provider or at the organizational level, determined by a system-wide policy. Maria's clinic, where is a patient, is affected by this reality.

Key ethical questions

1. How should Maria's clinic or physician decide who gets the available vaccine in an ethical manner?

2. What considerations should be factored into which populations ought to be prioritized?

3. Is this decision fair and equitable, or does it unfairly advantage some individuals?

4. How should personal values and professional obligations be balanced, and how does cost compared to clinical need play a role?

5. What are the immediate (patient) and extended (society) implications?

Ethical analysis

The decision to fairly allocate limited resources, particularly in a health care environment or organization, is especially challenging. The complexity of the situation is compounded by considering multiple factors: personal values of the clinicians, professional obligations to patients and customers, institutional policies and compliance that are expected to be enforced, the safety and risks of others that may be affected by extension of the decision (i.e., children, family members, co-workers, the public), and clinical or medical necessity. An additional practical layer of factors is of consideration with any organizational enterprise, namely cost and resources. There are several traditional approaches to this challenge:

- **The lottery method**. This model allows for chance to determine who receives the vaccine, based on a blinded system of selection. This approach offers a seemingly fair method of distribution, but it may inadvertently favor those who need the vaccine the least while simultaneously disadvantaging those who have most to benefit

- **First-come, first served**. Perhaps the most common and arguably fair method of distribution, this model favors those who take the initiative to seek out the vaccine based on their need and urgency. In an ideal situation, this approach would benefit those who require the vaccine with greatest urgency, yet in reality such efforts are predicted on the ability of a patient to access their provider in a timely manner. Given real-world challenges of time, money, work and family conflicts, and means of transportation, this model can disadvantage those with limited resources.

- **Clinical need**. Unlike the other two models, this approach seeks to prioritize the decision based on an objective measure. Allowing the health care provider to determine the need based on his or her professional discretion helps to limit the influence of implicit bias and external factors while relying on professional duty to the patient and society.

Outcome

The decision to fairly allocate vaccine supply was determine on a tiered model, weighted by population risk:

- The initial distribution of the vaccine was limited to those who were most susceptible to health risk: healthy children 2 years and older and healthy household members who have infants younger than six months of age

- The next tier was allocated to high-risk groups such as pregnant women, household members and caregivers for children younger than 6 months of age, health care professionals, and high-risk individuals with chronic medical conditions or comorbidities

- Given her risk category, Maria was placed in the "medical need" tier and was able to receive the vaccination before the general patient population of the same clinic. In a fair and equitable manner, this decision requires that Maria meets her ethical contractto appear on time for her vaccination

Questions for discussion

- How would the decision change if an at-risk elderly individual is unable to afford transport to the clinic?

- How might the decision change if a low-risk individual appeared first and offered to pay a premium amount for the vaccine? Does it change your decision knowing that this payment can be used to treat other (or more) patients in the clinic?

Conflict of interest

The authors declare no conflict of interest.

Author details

Josh Hyatt[1]* and Jeffrey Gruenglas[2]

1 Massachusetts College of Pharmacy and Health Sciences, Boston, Massachusetts, USA

2 Boston University, Boston, Massachusetts, USA

*Address all correspondence to: josh.hyatt@mcphs.edu

References

[1] Errida A, Lotfi B. The determinants of organizational change management success: Literature review and case study. International Journal of Engineering Business Management. 2021;**2021**:13. DOI: 10.1177/18479790211016273

[2] Rehman N, Mahmood A, Ibtasam M, Murtaza S, Iqbal N, Molnar E. The psychology of resistance to change: The antidotal effect of organizational justice, support and leader-member exchange. Frontiers in Psychology. 2021;**2021**:12. DOI: 10.3389/fpsyg.2021.678952/full

[3] Scholtens B, Dam L. Cultural values and international differences in business ethics. Journal of Business Ethics. 2007;**75**:273-284. DOI: 10.1007/s10551-006-9252-9

[4] Karabal C. Resistance to Change and Conflict of Interest: A Case Study. Vol. 2018. London, UK: Intech; 2017. DOI: 10.5772/intechopen.71578

[5] Pritlove C, Juando-Prats C, Ala-Leppilampi K, Parsons JA. The good, the bad, and the ugly of implicit bias. Lancet (London, England). 2019;**393**(10171):502-504. DOI: 10.1016/S0140-6736(18)32267-0

[6] Epley N, Kumar A. How to Design an Ethical Organization [Internet]. Harvard Business Review. 2019. Available from: https://hbr.org/2019/05/how-to-design-an-ethical-organization [Accessed: July 27, 2023]

[7] Norms V, Conditions H. An introduction. Journal of Human Values. 2019;**25**(1):vii-xi. DOI: 10.1177/0971685818806629

Chapter 3

Emotional Intelligence and Coping with Daily Stress in the Academic/Work Environment

Ana María Morales-Rodríguez and Francisco Manuel Morales-Rodríguez

Abstract

The COVID-19 pandemic has impacted the emotional dimension: its positive aspect and emotional regulation, as well as its negative internalized symptoms of stress, anxiety, and depression. This study's objective was to evaluate these emotional aspects and the most commonly employed strategies for coping with daily stress and facing conflicts in the academic/work environment in a sample of university students. For this, a cross-sectional quantitative design was used. Instruments were administered to evaluate these constructs, whose interrelationships were made known, by pointing out the importance of designing programs for providing training on coping, that focused on emotions in the university environment.

Keywords: emotional intelligence, social skills, coping, university happiness, conflict

1. Introduction

Coping is defined by Lazarus and Folkman [1] as "constantly changing cognitive and behavioral efforts to manage specific external and/or internal demands, that are appraised as taxing or exceeding the resources of the person."

In a recent systematic review, González Moreno and Molero [2], examined the various coping strategies used in the face of social conflicts and found that seeking social support was the most appropriate strategy for coping with daily stress. Similarly, other studies such as Rodriguez et al. [3] found that social support and problem solving were among the adequate coping strategies employed. Likewise, Coban [4] found that problem solving and social support were functional coping strategies employed by Turkish students.

The use of productive or functional coping strategies is associated with higher levels of psychological adjustment [5–7].

The university environment is one of the areas that can generate more stress among young people [8–10], especially during the pandemic [6]. Hernández de la Hera et al. [8], in the research led by Dr. Morales, evaluated a sample of a total of 276 university students averaging 19.92 years old, most of them female, that were given tools to evaluate mathematic anxiety, attitude toward mathematics, general self-efficacy and attitudes toward statistics: (1) scale of attitude toward mathematics [11]; (2) scale of attitude toward statistics [11]; (3) scale for assessing math anxiety in secondary education (SAMAS) [12]; (4) general self-efficacy scale (EAG) [13, 14]. They found that anxiety (be it anxiety before the exams or anxiety toward learning mathematics and statistics in general) was predictive of the variable attitudes toward mathematics and statistics. Using an artificial intelligence-based analysis with the creation of an artificial neural network, it was also found that the general self-efficacy variable had a positive impact on the dependent variable attitudes toward mathematics and the variable attitudes toward statistics. The same results were also obtained for the sample of secondary education students who took part in this study.

Another study was carried out in the same year by Martínez et al. [9], where a sample composed of 290 participants took part. This study had the aim of examining the possible relations that existed between the variables self-esteem, stress levels, resilience, and coping skills by using an artificial intelligence-based model with instruments such as (1) ad hoc sociodemographic questionnaire; (2) Rosenberg Self-Esteem Scale designed by Rosenberg [15], (3) Spanish version of the Perceived Stress Scale (PSS) [16, 17]; and (4) Brief Resilient Coping Scale [18]. It designed an algorithm capable of predicting self-esteem levels based on the variables of resilience, coping mechanisms, and other sociodemographic variables. In this study, which used an *ex post facto* design, the findings were that both the perceived levels of stress and resilience were variables with predictive ability over the self-esteem variable. This leads us to consider the importance of training in healthy coping strategies in early childhood education [19].

Other previous studies have also shown that the academic context can be one of the contexts that generate stress and anxiety in university students [20]. Morales and Morales-Rodríguez [20] assessed anxiety levels in a sample of 203 university students from the Faculties of Psychology and the Faculty of Education Science, most of them female, who were given a State-Trait Anxiety Inventory (STAI) [21, 22] as an instrument, in which they found that fourth-year undergraduate students had higher levels of anxiety compared to students in lower years, although they did not find statistically significant differences in anxiety levels according to gender.

The following is an analysis of two recent studies which show that in order to promote adequate psychological adjustment and social and academic adaptation, it is necessary for psychoeducational intervention programs to include variables such as the promotion of resilience and the appropriate use of stress coping mechanisms that allow for adequate emotional management in university students and future teachers to avoid situations of burnout and maladjustment [23, 24].

Moreno-Lucas [23] in a sample of 401 participants of whom the majority (70.6%) were women, were given an instrument to assess burnout (Maslach Burnout Inventory (MBI)) [25], Spanish version by Salanova et al. [26], and another to assess resilient coping (Brief Resilience Coping Scale (BRCS), scale by Sinclair et al. [27] and adapted to Spanish [28]). It was found that the resilience variable correlated inversely with variables such as emotional exhaustion and stress in this sample of participants. Along the same lines, Martínez-Ramón et al. [23] carried out a study in which they demonstrated the need to take into account the effects of variables such as gender when assessing these dimensions and found statistically significant differences in the variable emotional exhaustion according to gender. Specifically, in this study [23], higher scores were found in the emotional exhaustion variable in women compared to men.

Another research was carried out by Morales [29], in which a sample of subjects participated with the main objective of examining whether there were relationships between the coping strategies variable and other constructs such as emotional intelligence and social skills variables. For this purpose, after the corresponding request from the Ethics Committee of the institution, the following instruments were used: (1) Social Skills Questionnaire by Torbay, Munoz de Bustillo, and Hernández [30]; (2) Multidimensional Self-Concept Scale (AF-5) by García and Musitu [31]; (3) Coping Scale (CS) by Morales et al. [32], and (4) Trait Meta-Mood Scale (TMMS-24) [33] to assess emotional intelligence adapted by Fernández-Berrocal et al. [34]. In this study [29], the following most relevant results were found: (a) the existence of statistically significant relationships between the functional coping strategies variable and the emotional intelligence variable; (b) statistically significant correlations between the productive coping strategies variable and the social skills construct; and (c) statistically significant correlations between effective or adaptive coping strategies and the academic self-concept variable in the sample of participants in this study. Also, direct positive effects were found for some of the dimensions of the self-concept variable and the social skills variable on strategies considered as productive coping strategies, such as the "information seeking" strategy. This study [29] already indicated the importance of continuing with studies that are increasingly emerging in which mindfulness is taken into account in some way with the appropriate self-knowledge and management of emotions.

Precisely, as indicated at the end of the previous paragraph, it is of interest to focus on some of the studies that deal with the possible relationships between emotional skills and mindfulness. In the work of Moscoso [35], it is shown that emotional intelligence mediates between mindfulness and the increase of positive emotions, with the benefits that this entails for people's well-being. It is also indicated in this review [35] of literature in Educational Sciences and Psychology that the practice of mindfulness can contribute to the improvement of people's emotional skills. We are referring to the term mindfulness as "the practice of intentionally focusing attention on the present moment without making value judgements" (Kabat-Zinn [36], cited in Moscoso [35]). Moscoso and Legancher [37] also point out in this review of scientific literature that in mindfulness, two components can be distinguished that are involved in some way in the process of emotional regulation and changes in the individual's perception, such as the following elements:

1. Minimizing value judgments;

2. Self-regulating attention in the present moment.

Moscoso [35] also states in this literature review that it is the "sustaining of attention" in the emotions and thoughts of the experience of the present moment, an important aspect from a model centered on mindfulness, that influences the regulation of emotions.

Along these lines, research by Teal et al. [38] also shows that both mindfulness and emotional intelligence are constructs that tend to be present in one way or another in programs to improve people's well-being. Specifically, in their research [38], they examined the relationships between emotional intelligence, dispositional mindfulness, and well-being in a sample of 294 individuals aged between 13 and 17 years who were administered the following assessment instruments:

1. The SUEIT-A/the Adolescent Swinburne University Emotional Intelligence Scale (SUEIT-A) instrument by Luebbers et al. [39] consists of four subscales for the assessment of emotional intelligence: (a) Emotional Management and Control, (b) Emotions Direct Cognition, (c) Understanding the Emotions of Others, and (d) Emotional Recognition and Expression.

2. Lyubomirsky and Lepper's SHS instrument, the Subjective Happiness Scale [40] to assess the Happiness construct. It is a scale with adequate psychometric properties of reliability and validity.

3. The General Health Questionnaire (GHQ-12) by Goldberg and Hillier [41] for the assessment of Psychological distress.

4. The Mindfulness Attention Awareness Scale for Adolescents (MAAS-A) by Brown et al. [42].

In this study [38], statistically significant positive correlations between the dispositional mindfulness variable and the subjective happiness variable were found. In contrast, the results of this study [38] showed statistically significant inverse correlations between the dispositional mindfulness variable and the psychological distress variable. This result, as also shown in this study, is congruent with other previous research in which negative correlations are also found between dispositional mindfulness and mood disorders such as anxiety and depression [43]. Similarly, another study [44] focused on investigating how adaptive emotion regulation and mindfulness might affect adjustment to stressful situations in the transition to university in a sample of 158 undergraduate students at the University of Connecticut, 80% of whom were female and who completed online surveys at the beginning and end of their first semester. Specifically, they completed the Cognitive and Affective Mindfulness Scale-Revised (CAMS-R) from [45], The Difficulties in Emotion Regulation Scale (DERS) from [46], The Depression, Anxiety, and Stress Scales (DASS-21) from [47], and The FACIT-Sp-Non-Illness version [48, 49] which allows for the assessment of Spiritual well-being, finding statistically significant positive correlations between the adaptive regulation of emotions and the well-being variable.

In the work of Azpiazu et al. [50], the relationships between social support and emotional intelligence were studied in a large sample of 1543 subjects aged between 11 and 18 years, 52.81% of whom were female, using as instruments the Teacher and Classmate Support Scale of the Health Behavior in School-aged Children by Torsheim et al. [51]; the Trait Meta-Mood Scale-24 (TMMS-24) emotional intelligence scale, which is the same as the one used in our study and was adapted by Fernández-Berrocal et al. [52]; and another instrument to assess social support, the Family and Friends Support Questionnaire (AFA), by González and Landero [53]. In this study [50], the social support variable was found to be a relevant variable with predictive capacity for the emotional intelligence variable in both the sample of women and the sample of men. Specifically, in the sample of men, the results showed that emotional support was one of the variables with the highest predictive capacity for adequate emotional regulation, while support from friends was the factor with the highest predictive capacity on the dimensions of the emotional intelligence construct called the clarity of feelings and emotional attention in the sample of men.

Conversely, in the female sample, the results of this study [50] show that family support is the variable that most predicts emotional clarity and emotional regulation, while peer support such as friends is the one that most predicts the subdimension of emotional intelligence construct called emotional attention. Thus, the importance of the main agent of primary socialization, the family, and the main agent of secondary socialization, the school, is evident in this study.

Precisely, the present study's aim was to evaluate the coping strategies used by a sample of university students to deal with conflicts in the academic/work environment, and its possible relationship with the emotional intelligence variable.

2. Methods

2.1 Participants

The participants were 73 university students. The majority were women between the ages of 18 and 24 years.

2.2 Instruments

Coping Strategies Inventory (CSI) [54]; adaptation in Spanish Cano-García et al. [55].

It is a scale consisting of 40 items with a Likert-type response format. It has adequate psychometric properties of reliability and validity, with its α ranging from 0.75 to 0.88. An example of an instrument item is: "I coped with the problem."

Trait Meta-Mood Scale (TMM-24); Fernández-Berrocal et al. [56] for the assessment of emotional intelligence. It consists of 24 items with a five-step Likert-type response format. It has adequate psychometric properties ($\alpha = 0.90$). An example of this scale's item is: "I pay a lot of attention to feelings."

2.3 Procedure

The questionnaires were administered collectively in the different classrooms. This study received a favorable report from the University of Granada's Ethics Committee in Human Sciences. Anonymity and confidentiality of the information were guaranteed after obtaining the consent of the study's participants.

2.4 Data design and analysis

A quantitative design was used. Descriptive analyses and bivariate correlation analyses were performed to analyze the relationship between the variables.

3. Results

With respect to the results, it can be highlighted when the students were specifically asked about a problem in their academic or work environment, and their most used coping strategies were: solving the problem and seeking social support. Specifically, for the active solution strategy, the mean was 15.47, and standard deviation was 3.37; for social support, the mean was 15.37, and standard deviation was 3.59; for emotional expression, the mean was 13.7 and standard deviation was 4.24; for self-criticism, the mean was 12.46 and standard deviation 3.9; for cognitive restructuring, the mean was 13.68 and standard deviation 3.77; for problem avoidance, the mean was

10.94 and standard deviation 4.33; and finally for social withdrawal, the mean was 11.15 and standard deviation 3.67.

Regarding the relationship between the study variables, it can be highlighted that statistically significant positive correlations were found between the total scores in the use of coping strategies in the face of work-related problems and the emotional intelligence variable in this sample of university students ($r = .47, p < .01$).

4. Discussion and conclusions

This study's aim was to evaluate the strategies most frequently used in the work/academic environment by university students for coping with daily stress. Likewise, the relationships between the variables, strategies for coping with stress in the face of work or academic conflicts, and emotional intelligence were analyzed.

When faced with a problem in the academic and/or work environment, problem solving, and social support were the coping strategies most frequently employed by the present sample.

These are coping strategies considered a priori as productive or functional [32]. Likewise, another study [57] found that the problem-solving strategy is one of the most commonly used coping strategies in certain situations of daily stress.

The results show the existence of statistically significant associations between the total scores of the various coping strategies for academic/work stress and emotional intelligence. This result can be considered congruent with other previous studies that highlight the importance of emotional intelligence, given its possible relationship with the use of one or another coping strategy [58], as well as its implications for educators, as indicated by Mayer and Salovey's model [59].

Other theoretical models that are somehow in line with the results obtained in this study can also be found. For instance, the model reflected in the study carried out by Downey et al. [60] points to the existence of links between coping strategies and the intrapersonal emotional intelligence variable, which may become one of the relevant psychoeducational variables for the adequate management of everyday stress and adversity in children and young people. By the same token, in the research carried out by Wang et al. [61], they found that self-efficacy was a mediating variable between active coping with stress and emotional intelligence.

A limitation of this study to be noted is that it was a cross-sectional study. It is also necessary to continue expanding the sample. Additionally, as a future line of research, the relationships with other psychoeducational variables or constructs could be analyzed. For example, applying other questionnaires validated more specifically in the Spanish context, such as the questionnaire adapted by Munduate et al. [62] to assess interpersonal conflict management style and its relationships with the typology of coping strategies for coping with daily stress. Possible relationships could also be analyzed using a more complex multivariate model with the mindfulness variable, as in the study by Pérez-Yus et al. [63].

5. Conclusions

It can be concluded that conflict resolution and social support were the strategies used by the present sample for coping with daily stress in the academic/work environment.

The information obtained in this research is considered useful for designing training actions and programs for the prevention of daily stress, especially considering that fewer studies have evaluated the scores of coping strategies most used in the face of daily stress problems in the work or academic environment, compared to other conflicts or major problems.

Author details

Ana María Morales-Rodríguez[1] and Francisco Manuel Morales-Rodríguez[2*]

1 University of Málaga, Málaga, Spain

2 University of Granada, Granada, Spain

*Address all correspondence to: fmmorales@ugr.es

References

[1] Lazarus RS, Folkman RS. Stress Appraisal and Coping. New York, NY: Springer Publishing Company; 1984

[2] González-Moreno A, Molero-Jurado MM. Coping strategies in conflicts among adolescents: A systematic review. REMIE: Multidisciplinary Journal of Educational Research. 2022;**12**(2):146-170

[3] Rodríguez FJ, Ovejero A, Bringas C, Moral MV. Conflict coping in adolescent socialization. Proposal of a model. Psychology from the Caribbean. 2016;**33**(1):1-13. Available from: https://rcientificas.uninorte.edu.co/index.php/psicologia/article/view/6895

[4] Çoban AE. Interpersonal cognitive distortions and stress coping strategies of late adolescents. Egitim Arastirmalari – Eurasian Journal of Education and Research. 2013;**51**:65-84. Available from: http://ejer.com.tr/public/assets/catalogs/0926220001556187670.pdf

[5] Morales-Rodríguez FM. Risk suicide, anxiety, and coping strategies. In: Suicide. London, UK: IntechOpen; 2021. DOI: 10.5772/intechopen.99618

[6] Morales-Rodríguez FM, Martínez-Ramón JP, Méndez I, Ruiz-Esteban C. Stress, coping, and resilience before and after COVID-19: A predictive model based on artificial intelligence in the university environment. Frontiers in Psychology. 2021;**12**:647964. DOI: 10.3389/fpsyg.2021.647964

[7] Morales-Rodríguez FM, Pérez-Mármol JM. The role of anxiety, coping strategies, and emotional intelligence on general perceived self-efficacy in university students. Frontiers in Psychology. 2019;**10**:1689. DOI: 10.3389/fpsyg.2019.01689

[8] Hernándezde la Hera JM, Morales-Rodríguez FM, Rodríguez-Gobiet JP, Martínez-Ramón JP. Attitudes toward mathematics/statistics, anxiety, self-efficacy and academic performance: An artificial neural network. Frontiers in Psychology. 2023;**14**:1214892. DOI: 10.3389/fpsyg.2023.1214892

[9] Martínez-Ramón JP, Morales-Rodríguez FM, Ruiz-Esteban C, Méndez I. Self-esteem at university: Proposal of an artificial neural network based on resilience, stress, and sociodemographic variables. Frontiers in Psychology. 2022;**13**:815853. DOI: 10.3389/fpsyg.2022.815853

[10] Morales Rodríguez FM, Martínez Ramón JP, Corvace C, Morales Rodríguez AM. Uso de las estrategias de afrontamiento en la adolescencia: Un estudio preliminar de las diferencias de género. *Acción psicológica* 2023 (Ejemplar dedicado a: Desafíos y estrategias de intervención en la adolescencia: un enfoque multidimensional). 2023:21-32

[11] Auzmendi E. Las actitudes hacia la matemática-estadística en las enseñanzas medias y universitarias. Bilbao: Mensajero; 1992

[12] Yáñez-Marquina L, Villardón-Gallego L. Math anxiety, a hierarchical construct: Development and validation of the scale for assessing math anxiety in secondary education. Anxiety Stress. 2017;**23**:59-65. DOI: 10.1016/j.anyes.2017.10.001

[13] Baessler J, Schwarzer R. Evaluación de la autoeficacia; Adaptación española de la escala de autoeficacia general

[Assessing self-efficacy: Spanish adaption of the general self-efficacy scale]. Ansiedad Estrés. 1996;**2**:1-8

[14] Espada JP, Gonzálvez MT, Orgilés M, Carballo JL, Piqueras JA. Validación de la escala de autoeficacia general con adolescentes españoles [Validation of the general self-efficacy scale in Spanish teenagers]. Electronic Journal of Research in Educational Psychology. 2012;**10**:355-370. DOI: 10.25115/ejrep.v10i26.1504

[15] Rosenberg M. Rosenberg self-esteem scale (RSE): Acceptance and commitment therapy. Measures Package. 1965;**61**:52

[16] Cohen S, Kamarck T, Mermelstein R. A global measure of perceived stress. Journal of Health and Social Behavior. 1983;**24**:385-396. DOI: 10.2307/2136404

[17] Remor E. Psychometric properties of a European Spanish version of the perceived stress scale (PSS). The Spanish Journal of Psychology. 2006;**9**:86-93. DOI: 10.1017/s1138741600006004

[18] Ceballos-Ospino GA, Paba-Barbosa C, Suescún J, Oviedo HC, Herazo E, Campo Arias A. Validez y dimensionalidad de la escala de autoestima de Rosenberg en estudiantes universitarios. Pensamiento Psicológico. 2017;**15**:29-39. DOI: 10.11144/javerianacali.ppsi15-2.vdea

[19] Morales-Rodríguez FM, Martínez-Ramón JP, Narváez Peláez MA, Corvasce C. Understanding school anxiety in Italian adolescence through an artificial neural network: Influence of social skills and coping strategies. Children. 2023;**10**:1688. DOI: 10.3390/children10101688

[20] Morales Rodríguez FM, Morales Rodríguez AM. Diferencias en ansiedad en función del curso en universitarios. Revista INFAD De Psicología. International Journal of Developmental and Educational Psychology. 2021;**1**(1):303-308 https://doi.org/10.17060/ijodaep.2021.n1.v1.2067

[21] Fonseca-Pedrero E, Paino M, Sierra-Baigrie S, Lemos-Giráldez S, Muñiz J. PropiedadesPsicométricas del "Cuestionario de Ansiedad Estado-Rasgo" (STAI) en Universitarios [PsychometricProperties of the "state-trait anxiety questionnaire"]. Behavioral Psychology/Psicología Conductual. 2012;**20**:547-561

[22] Spielberger CD, Gorsuch RL, Lushene RE, Cubero NS. STAI: Cuestionario de ansiedad estadorasgo. TEA Ediciones: Madrid, España; 2011

[23] Martínez-Ramón JP, Morales-Rodríguez FM, Pérez-López S, Méndez Mateo I, Ruiz-Esteban C. Predicción de la resiliencia docente mediante redes neuronales artificiales: influencia del burnout y del estrés por COVID-19. Anales de Psicología/Annals of Psychology. 2023;**39**(1):100-111. DOI: 10.6018/analesps.515611

[24] Moreno-LucasJL,Martínez-RamónJP, Morales-Rodríguez FM, Ruiz-Esteban C, Méndez EI. Stress, burnout, and resilience: Are teachers at risk? International Journal of Mental Health Promotion. 2023;*25*(2):207-222. DOI: 10.32604/ijmhp.2023.025901

[25] Maslach C, Jackson SE. The measurement of experienced burnout. Journal of Organizational Behavior. 1981;**2**(2):99-113. DOI: 10.1002/(ISSN)1099-1379

[26] Salanova M, Schaufeli WB, Llorens S, Peiro JM, Grau R. From burnout to engagement: A new perspective? Journal of Work and

Organizational Psychology. 2000;**16**(2):117-134

[27] Sinclair VG, Wallston KA. The development and psychometric evaluation of the brief resilient coping scale. Assessment. 2004;**11**(1):94-101. DOI: 10.1177/1073191103258144

[28] Moret-Tatay C, Fernández-Muñoz JJ, Civera-Mollá C, Navarro-Pardo E, Alcover-de-la-Hera C. Propiedades psicométricas y estructura factorial del BRCS en una muestra de personas mayores españolas. Anales de Psicología/ Annals of Psychology. 2015;**31**(3):1030-1034. DOI: 10.6018/analesps.31.3.188401

[29] Morales FM. Relaciones entre el afrontamiento del estrés cotidiano, autoconcepto, habilidades sociales e inteligencia emocional [relationships between coping with daily stress, self-concept, social skills and emotional intelligence]. The European Journal of Psychology of Education. 2017;**10**:41-48. DOI: 10.1016/j.ejeps.2017.04.001

[30] Torbay A, Muñoz de Bustillo M, Hernández C. Los estudiantes universitarios de carreras asistenciales: Qué habilidades interpersonales dominan y cuáles creen necesarias para su future profesional. Aula Abierta. 2001;**78**:1-17

[31] García F, Musitu G. AF5: Autoconcepto Forma 5: Manual. Madrid: Publicaciones de Psicología Aplicada, TEA Ediciones; 2001

[32] Morales-Rodríguez FM, Trianes-Torres MV, Blanca-Mena MJ, Miranda-Páez J, Escobar-Espejo M, Fernández-Baena FJ. Escala de afrontamiento en niños: propiedades psicométricas [Coping scale in children: Psychometric properties]. Anales de Psicología. 2012;**28**(2):475-483. DOI: 10.6018/analesps.28.2.136221

[33] Salovey P, Mayer JD, Goldman S, Turvey C, Palfai T. Emotional attention, clarity and repair: Exploring emotional intelligence using the trait mood scale. In: Pennebaker JW, editor. Emotion, Disclosure and Health. WashingtonDC: American Psychological Association; 1995. pp. 125-154

[34] Fernández-Berrocal P, Extremera N, Ramos N. Inteligencia emocional y depresión. Encuentros en Psicología Social. 2003;**1**(5):251-254

[35] Moscoso M. Hacia una Integración de mindfulness e inteligencia emocional en psicología y educación. *LIBERABIT*. Revista Peruana De Psicología. 2019, 2019;**25**(1):107-117. DOI: 10.24265/liberabit.2019.v25n1.09

[36] Kabat-Zinn J. Full Catastrophe Living: Using the Wisdom of your Body and Mind to Face Stress, Pain, and Illness. New York: Dell Publishing; 1990

[37] Moscoso MS, Lengacher CA. Mecanismos neurocognitivos de la terapia basada en mindfulness. Liberabit. 2015;**21**(2):221-233

[38] Teal C, Downey LA, Lomas JE, Ford TC, Bunnett ER, Stough C. The role of dispositional mindfulness and emotional intelligence in adolescent males. Mindfulness. 2018;**10**(1):159-167. DOI: 10.1007/s12671-018-0962-8

[39] Luebbers S, Downey LA, Stough C. The development of an adolescent measure of EI. Personality and Individual Differences. 2007;**42**(6):999-1009. DOI: https://doi.org/10.1016/j.paid.2006. 09.009

[40] Lyubomirsky S, Lepper HS. A measure of subjective happiness: Preliminary reliability and construct validation. Social Indicators Research. 1999;**46**(2):137-155. DOI: 10.1023/a:1006824100041

[41] Goldberg DP, Hillier VF. A scaled version of the general health questionnaire. Psychological Medicine. 1979;**9**(1):139-145

[42] Brown KW, West AM, Loverich TM, Biegel GM. Assessing adolescent mindfulness: Validation of an adapted mindful attention awareness scale in adolescent normative and psychiatric populations. Psychological Assessment. 2011;**23**(4):1023-1033. DOI: 10.1037/a0021338

[43] Brown KW, Ryan RM. The benefits of being present: Mindfulness and its role in psychological well-being. Journal of Personality and Social Psychology. 2003;**84**(4):822-848

[44] Finkelstein-Fox L, Park CL, Riley KE. Mindfulness and emotion regulation: Promoting well-being during the transition to college. Anxiety, Stress, and Coping. 2018;**31**(6):639-653. DOI: 10.1080/10615806.2018.1518635

[45] Feldman G, Hayes A, Kumar S, Greeson J, Laurenceau J-P. Mindfulness and emotion regulation: The development and initial validation of the cognitive and affective mindfulness scale-revised (CAMS-R). Journal of Psychopathology and Behavioral Assessment. 2007;**29**:177-190

[46] Gratz KL, Roemer L. Multidimensional assessment of emotion regulation and dysregulation: Development, factor structure, and initial validation of the difficulties in emotion regulation scale. Journal of Psychopathology and Behavioral Assessment. 2004;**26**:41-54

[47] Lovibond SH, Lovibond PF. Manual for the Depression Anxiety Stress Scales. 2nd ed. Sydney: Psychology Foundation; 1995

[48] Bredle JM, Salsman JM, Debb SM, Arnold BJ, Cella D. Spiritual well-being as a component of healthrelated quality of life: The functional assessment of chronic illness therapy—Spiritual well-being scale (FACIT-Sp). Religions. 2011;**2**:77-94

[49] Peterman AH, Fitchett G, Brady MJ, Hernandez L, Cella D. Measuring spiritual well-being in people with cancer: The functional assessment of chronic illness therapy—Spiritual well-being scale (FACIT-Sp). Annals of Behavioral Medicine. 2002;**24**:49-58

[50] Azpiazu L, Esnaola I, Sarasa M. Capacidad predictivadel apoyo social en la inteligencia emocional. European Journal of Education and Psychology. 2015;**8**:23-29. DOI: 10.1016/j.ejeps.2015.10.003

[51] Torsheim T, Wold B, y Samdal, O. The teacher and classmate support scale: Factor structure, test-retest reliability and validity in samples of 13 and 15 year adolescents. School Psychology International. 2000;**21**(2):195-212

[52] Fernández-Berrocal P, Alcaide R, Domínguez E, Fernández-McNally C, Ramos NS, Ravira M. Adaptación al castellano de la escala rasgo de metaconocimiento sobre estados emocionales de Salovey et al.: datos preliminares. Vol. 1. En Libro de actas del V Congreso de Evaluación Psicológica; 1998. pp. 83-84

[53] González MT, Landero R. Síntomas psicosomáticos y estrés: comparación de un modelo estructural entre hombres y mujeres. Ciencia UANL. 2008;**11**(4):403-410

[54] Tobin DL, Holroyd KA, Reynolds RV, Kigal JK. The hierarchicalfactor structure of the coping strategies inventory.

Cognitive Therapy and Research. 1989;**13**:343-361

[55] Cano-García FJC, Franco LR, Martínez JG. Spanish adaptation of the coping strategies inventory. Actas Españolas de Psiquiatría. 2007;**35**:29-39. Available from: https://www.researchgate.net/publication/235419673_Adaptacion_Espanola_del_Invent

[56] Fernández-Berrocal P, Extremera N, Ramos N. Validity and reliability of the Spanish modified version of the trait meta-mood scale. Psychological Reports. 2004;**94**:751-755

[57] Morales FM, Trianes MV. Coping in Childhood: Assessment and Relationships with Psychological Adjustment. Madrid, Spain: Aljibe; 2012

[58] Morales-Rodríguez FM, Trianes-Torres MV, Miranda-Páez J, Inglés CJ. Prevalence of strategies for coping with daily stress in children. Psicothema. 2016;**28**(4):370-376. DOI: 10.7334/psic othema2015.10

[59] Mayer JD, Salovey P. What is emotional intelligence? In: Salovey P, Sluyter D, editors. Emotional Development and Emotional Intelligence: Implications for Educators. New York: Basic Books; 1997. pp. 3-31

[60] Downey L, Johnston P, Hansen K, Birney J, Stough, C. Investigating the mediating effects of emotional intelligence and coping on problem behaviours inadolescents. Australian Journal of Psychology. 2010;**62**:20-29. DOI: 10.1080/00049530903312873

[61] Wang Y, Xie G, Cui X. Effects of emotional intelligence and self-leadership on students' coping with stress. Social Behavior and Personality. 2016;**44**:853-864. DOI: 10.2224/sbp.2016.44.5.853

[62] Munduate L, Ganaza J, Alcaide M. Conflict management styles in organizations. Revista de Psicologia Social. 1993;**8**(1):47-68. DOI: 10.1080/02134748.1993.10821669

[63] Pérez-Yus MC, Ayllón-Negrillo E, Delsignore G, Magallón-Botaya R, Aguilar-Latorre A, Oliván-Blázquez B. Variables associated with negotiation effectiveness: The role of mindfulness. Frontiers in Psychology. 2020;**11**:1214. DOI: 10.3389/fpsyg.2020.01214

Chapter 4

Changes in Mindfulness Attitude after Parent–Child Interaction Therapy Skills Acquisition: Comparison of Mindfulness Attitude before and after the Parent–Child Interaction Therapy 40 Hours Basic Training

Tomoko Kuniyoshi

Abstract

I conducted this study to verify that the acquisition of PRIDE skills, an important skill for building good parent–child relationships in parent–child interaction therapy (PCIT), is associated with mindfulness attitude formation. PCIT, which was developed by Eyberg in 1974, is a behavioral therapy based on play therapy in which a therapist provides live coaching from a separate room while parents and children are playing in the same room to improve the parent–child relationship and children's problem behaviors. The original and unique feature of my study is that I discussed PRIDE skills and mindfulness from the perspective that both are related to attentional control functions. The mindful attention awareness scale (MAAS) Japanese version was used as a measure of mindfulness. I compared the MAAS score of seven graduates who mastered PRIDE skills before and after 40 hours of PCIT International Prescribed Training Workshop, and as a control group, I compared the MAAS score of six non-training participants. As a result, the MAAS score had a significantly decreased tendency only in the PCIT group. It was suggested that mindfulness tendency may have increased in the PCIT group. PCIT may contribute to mindfulness attitude formation through improved attention and awareness. This study was approved and conducted by the Ethics Committee of the Faculty of Human Sciences, Kobe College. There are no conflicts of interest.

Keywords: PCIT, mindfulness, PRIDE skills, MAAS, attention control, small-group comparative study

1. Introduction

I conducted this study to examine how the acquisition of skills for improving parent–child relationships (PRIDE skills) in PCIT: parent–child interaction therapy, promotes mindfulness attitude formation. This chapter presents the results of this study. Although studies on PCIT and mindfulness have existed to date, there are studies that argue against the two, as to whether PCIT or mindfulness techniques are more effective in improving caregivers' mental stability and children's problem behaviors (e.g., [1, 2]). I have not been able to find a study, at least at this time, that attempts to link PCIT and mindfulness in terms of "attentional functioning" by focusing on the similarities between the two functions, as my study does.

First, this is a unique perspective of this study. This study is only a comparative study with a very small sample. However, this study does indicate the possibility that the ability of skill users to observe and continuously verbalize their children's behavior tends to enhance the mindfulness attitudes of the users.

In this chapter, I begin by providing an overview of PCIT and the "PRIDE skills" used in the first half of PCIT, child directed interaction (CDI), which is an important premise for this study to facilitate the reader's understanding. PRIDE skills are a powerful tool for improving the relationship between caregivers and children and are one of the key components of this study. Therefore, I will first explain the skills and then provide a brief description of mindfulness. Next, I present the purpose, methods, results, and discussion of this study. This is because a basic understanding of PCIT and mindfulness is essential to the structure of this study.

Through this study, the reader will understand that the psychological functions embodied in the PRIDE skills of PCIT are related to mindful parenting attitudes. Furthermore, I believe that through this study, I was able to articulate the very abstract attitude of mindful parenting as a concrete behavior in the form of the PRIDE skills and provide a course of action that will help increase the practicability of mindful attitude formation for caregivers.

2. Outline of PCIT

2.1 What is PCIT?

Imagine a mother and her child happily playing together in a certain small playroom. The room is equipped with a one-way mirror, and a therapist in an adjacent observation room speaks to the mother wearing earphones, "Let's praise the child, saying, 'You built a wonderful castle'." The mother repeats the therapist's words and says to the child at her side, "You made a lovely castle." The praised child smiles at the mother and concentrates on playing again, building more and more gorgeous castles. The mother's face lights up as she sees her child smiling and concentrating on his play. The therapist says, "Mother, you did very well with your labeled praise!" and praises the mother for her efforts.

This is a typical scene at PCIT. A first-time observer would have no idea that this child has been diagnosed with ADHD and that just a few weeks ago, his mother was in trouble because of his terrible tantrums.

PCIT is a behavioral therapy based on play therapy in which a therapist provides live coaching from a separate room while parents and children are playing in the same room, as shown in **Figure 1**, to improve the parent–child relationship and children's problem behaviors. PCIT was developed by Eyberg of the University of Florida in 1974. Findings that it is effective in reducing parental re-abuse rates to 20% [3] have increased the reputation of PCIT throughout the United States. After years of empirical research and refinement, PCIT has been reported to improve children's problem

Figure 1.
PCIT role play in practice (therapist is skill coaching the parent role).

behaviors, especially behavioral disorders such as externalizing aggressive behaviors [4], and meta-studies have also reported high efficacy [5]. Furthermore, it is ranked as a "well-established treatment" in the American Psychological Association's evidence-based treatment guidelines [6]. Van der Kolk, a world authority on trauma, promotes the practice of PCIT at his trauma center, and Putnam, a leading dissociation researcher, has recommended PCIT in a lecture in Japan as effective in treating trauma and preventing abuse in children.

As shown in **Figure 2**, PCIT has an extremely high efficacy rate of d = 1.65 [7], indicating that it is outstandingly effective compared to medication, CBT, or other psychotherapies.

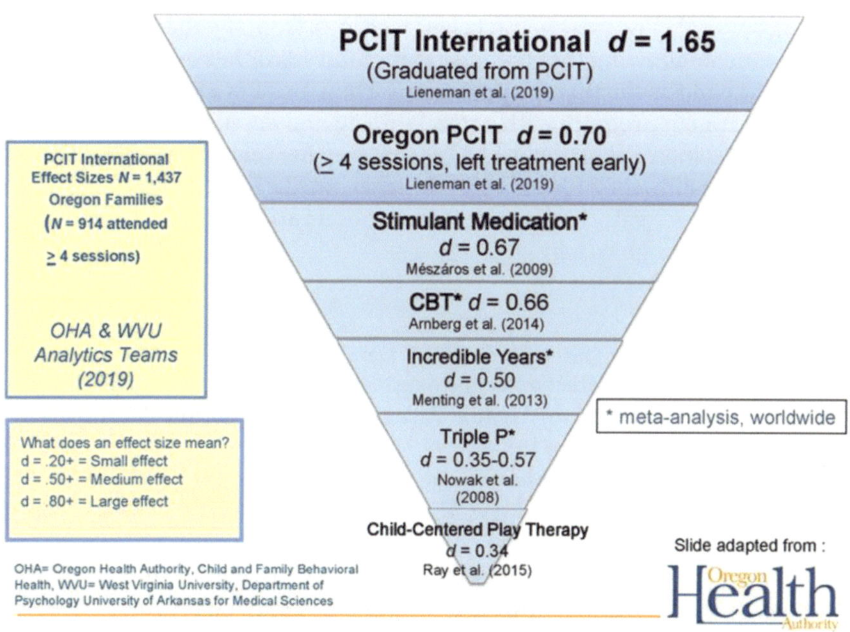

Figure 2.
Efficacy rates for each treatment. (Adapted from PCIT International Website: https://www.pcit.org/.)

PCIT is a behavioral therapy based on operant conditioning, but especially in the first half, it emphasizes the caregiver's receptive involvement in child-initiated play and stabilizing the psychological state of the child and parents by strengthening attachment relationships. As shown in the photo at the beginning of this article, PCIT uses a method whereby the therapist provides live coaching from a separate room to parents wearing earphones through a one-way mirror (or through a computer screen when using the Internet) and gives specific, direct advice to parents on how to interact with their children. The therapist does not directly intervene with the child, but rather, the parent is asked to engage with the child using good skills, and the therapist supports the parent in a nested structure. This way of having the caregivers themselves develop the skills to observe the child and intervene specifically is what makes PCIT unique. In this study, I focused on the PRIDE skills, which are acquired in the first half of the CDI and used by parents on a regular basis throughout the therapy and which are considered to be the most important skills for forming parent–child attachment and improving the good relationship.

2.2 Structure of PCIT: CDI and PDI

PCIT consists of two steps. The first half is CDI, and the second half is PDI (parent-directed interaction). As mentioned above, in the first half of the CDI, caregivers receive 30 minutes of coaching in each session to learn PRIDE skills (see below) and promote receptive interactions in order to rebuild the parent–child relationship. Then, caregivers move into PDI, where they learn how to appropriately control the child, including effective time-outs for modifying the child's behavior and how to give effective instructions. The extent of caregiver skill acquisition and improvement in the child's problem behavior is confirmed through assessment with the ECBI (Eyberg child behavior inventory) and DPICS (dyadic parent–child interaction coding system). The caregiver receives feedback from the therapist on the results of the assessment, allowing the caregiver to monitor his or her own growth and changes in the child as the therapy progresses. Thus, PCIT is a highly structured and systematic treatment program with a standardized and detailed protocol and manual. However, what is interesting about PCIT is that the therapist intervenes only with the caregiver and not directly with the child. In other words, PCIT is a training program for caregivers to practically improve their own observation skills and responsiveness to their children through coaching.

2.3 Skills in CDI

The PCIT descriptions presented in this paper are based on the PCIT Protocol [8] and the Abbreviated Manual for Dyadic Parent–Child Interaction Coding System, Clinical Manual Fourth Edition [9].

The goal for caregivers to achieve in the CDI is to master the PRIDE skills (Do skills) (**Table 1**) and eliminate the AVOID skills (Do not skills) (**Table 2**). The PCIT sets clear criteria for skill acquisition, and once caregivers have met those criteria, he or she can move on to the next stage, PDI. In CDI, the caregiver enters the playroom each time with the child and follows the child's lead in playing together. This time when the caregiver plays with the child using PRIDE skills and follows the child's lead is named "special play time," and the caregiver is given homework to practice the

PRIDE skills	Explanation and effects	Examples
P Labeled Praise	• Give children "Concrete praise" for positive behavior. • Increase praised behavior and boost the child's self-esteem.	"You picked a great color!" "You take good care of your pen!" "I'm glad you are playing quietly."
R Reflect	• Repeat the child's appropriate "words". • It allows the child to lead the conversation, shows that the parent is listening, and promotes the child's ability to speak.	Child: "I made a big castle!" Mother: "You made a big castle!" (A cat is sleeping nearby.) Child: "Cute cat!" Mother: "Cute cat taking a nap!"
I Imitate	• Imitate the appropriate "play or action" of the child. • Imitate has the function of focusing the parent on what the child is doing, allowing the child to lead the play.	If a child draws a tree, the parent draws a tree as well.
D Behavior Descriptions	• Explain appropriate child behavior. • Live coverage • BD can let the child know that the parent is interested in and paying attention to the child. Child can maintain attention to his or her activities.	A child has picked up a red crayon and is drawing an apple. Parent: "You have taken the red crayon and are drawing an apple."
E Enjoy	• Enjoying special play time with the child. • The parent can let the child know that he or she is enjoying time with the child.	Gentle body touch, laughter, and warm tone of voice to the child.

Partially modified from Kuniyoshi [10].

Table 1.
PRIDE skills.

skills at home by conducting "special play time" with the child for 5 minutes each day. In the playroom, the caregiver wears earphones and receives instructions from the therapist, who observes the parent and child through a one-way mirror, about their interactions as appropriate. Prior to each coaching session, the therapist conducts a 5-minute coding session to determine which of the caregiver's PRIDE skills are developing and which are weak and, based on the results, sets goals for each session and conducts coaching for approximately 30 minutes. The therapist also uses PRIDE skills throughout the therapy, talking to the caregiver, encouraging the caregiver, and consistently giving specific praise. In other words, PCIT cannot be successfully implemented unless the therapists themselves have mastered the PRIDE skills. The criteria for the mastery of PRIDE skills are discussed below.

<About PRIDE Skills>

PRIDE skills are the five skills listed in **Table 1** which are desirable skills for building parent–child relationships.

- **P (Labeled Praise)**: Specific praise for appropriate "behavior" of the child. (Praise helps children build self-esteem and feel accepted. The child learns what behavior is appropriate and will repeat positive behaviors.)

- **R (Reflect):** The caregiver repeats the child's appropriate utterances. (Reflect is a skill that allows the child to lead the conversation and promotes the child's ability to speak by showing the child that the caregiver is listening properly).

- **I (Imitate):** This is the skill of imitating the child's appropriate play (action). (Imitate allows the caregiver to focus on what the child is doing.)

- **D (Behavior Descriptions):** Describing the child's appropriate behavior. The caregiver provides a "play-by-play" account of the child's behavior as if the caregiver were an announcer (letting the child know that the caregiver is interested in and paying attention to the child). The child is able to maintain attention to his or her activities by having the caregiver's attention.

- **E (Enjoy):** Enjoying special times with the child. The caregiver acts happy and natural, letting the child know that he or she is enjoying the time with the child. This includes gentle body touches, laughter, and a tone of voice that indicates the caregiver's interest.

Thus, the five skills included in the PRIDE skills are those that make the child feel safe and secure in the sense that he or she is being watched and accepted with interest by the caregiver.

⟨Avoid Skills⟩

PRIDE skills are not the only skills in CDI. There are also another three skills, called "Avoid Skills," that can keep children away from negative influences by minimizing the use of these skills by the caregiver. The "avoid skills" consist of "Question," "Command," and "Negative Talk" (**Table 2**).

Avoid skills	Explanation and effects	Examples
Command Parent telling the child what he/she should or should not do.	CO takes the lead away from the child and causes him/her to lose the opportunity to make independent decisions.	⟨Indirect Command⟩ "Will you sit here?" "I think you should paint this one red." ⟨Direct Command⟩ "Please sit here." "Paint this part red."
Question Asking the child to give an answer.	QU lets the parent lead the conversation. Many questions are commands and demand answers.	"Why does this cow cry?" "Are you painting it red?" "Do you want to play with trains next?"
Negative Talk Expressions of disapproval toward the child.	It gives attention to inappropriate child behavior and lowers the child's self-esteem.	"You did not do so good." "Your paint just blew out. Oh, My God." "You could have painted it better." "Oh, no! You're going to paint that?" "That's why I warned you before!"

Partially modified from Kuniyoshi [10].

Table 2.
Avoid skills.

In addition to PRIDE and Do not skills, CDI also uses "Selective Attention" and "Active Ignoring" skills that do not give attention to the child's problem behavior, but since these skills are not directly addressed in this study, this paper will omit a description of these skills. In concluding my explanation of PCIT, I will discuss the standards for the mastery of PRIDE skills required of caregivers. This will be based on coding by DPICS. The caregiver uses each of the three verbal skills in the PRIDE skills, Labeled Praise, Reflection, and Behavior Description, at least 10 times in 5 minutes of play with the child and simultaneously uses the Do not skills no more than 3 times total in 5 minutes. In this study, the survey was conducted not with caregivers but with students attending a training workshop to become PCIT therapists. The reason for this will be explained later, but even in therapist training workshop, students are strongly expected to meet this mastery standard, and all participants in the PCIT therapist training workshop that I studied met this standard.

2.4 PCIT therapist training course and skill acquisition assessment

A prospective PCIT therapist must complete a 5-day, 40-hour training workshop in accordance with PCIT-International to accurately understand the principles, structure, and procedures of PCIT, as well as to acquire practical PRIDE skills. In this study, PRIDE skill acquisition was checked in the framework of DPICS skills coding for a 5-minute parent–child playtime video and a "mastery hour" of DPICS skills coding for a parent–child playtime role play. The mastery hour consisted of a 5-minute CDI role play in which the student played the parent and the trainer played the child, while another trainer and several students checked the skills of the student playing the parent based on DPICS. Thus, the mastery hour is a rigorous assessment of whether the student has met the mastery criteria. Participants in the parent role cannot complete the mastery hour exercise until they have fully met the prescribed PRIDE and Do not skills criteria in 5 minutes and must repeat the role play in the parent role until they reach the criteria. In this study, all trainees met these criteria, so all trainees were assigned to the mastery group.

2.5 Reasons for conducting this research with students in the training course

Since PCIT is a therapeutic technique for supporting caregivers, it is desirable that the study be conducted with caregivers who are actually receiving PCIT. However, even though PCIT is a short-term therapy, it often takes more than 20 sessions and about 6 months to complete. In addition, it is difficult to control the length of time because the time required for acquisition varies greatly from person to person, depending on the caregiver. Furthermore, at the facilities where I conduct PCIT, it is not possible to have many PCIT cases going on at the same time, and it is difficult to gather enough clients at the same time to actually study the effects of PCIT. For these reasons, it was decided to focus this study on participants in 40 hours training workshop, where several people can acquire skills under the same conditions in a short period of time.

3. About mindfulness

Mindfulness is a meditative state, so to speak, and according to Kabat-Zinn [11], mindfulness is defined as "paying attention in a particular way: on purpose, in the present moment, and nonjudgmentally." In recent years, mindfulness has been gaining attention as an essential component of mental health in various psychotherapies, including cognitive therapy, dialectical cognitive-behavioral therapy, and stress reduction methods. In mindfulness, the greatest emphasis is placed on the attitude of simply observing thoughts that arise within oneself "as they are." This is the process of "de-centering" through "awareness." For example, when negative thoughts are repeated, a mindfulness attitude can be helpful in curbing the vicious cycle of ruminating, as described by Segal et al. [12]. According to Segal et al. [12], in cognitive-behavioral therapy, mindfulness attitude is a process of "de-centering" that separates and "distances" the self from thoughts and feelings, which is closely related to procedures that promote contextual change and have a preventive effect on depression relapse. Mindfulness is the Pali word "sati," meaning "awareness," and according to Gunaratana [13], this state is a subtle work of the mind, beyond words and logic, but experiential. When we recognize something, the moment just before we identify it is the state of awareness. At the same time, he also points out that "awareness" means to see things from a broader perspective.

Sumanasara [14] provides an understandable summary of the commentary on the meditative states in early Theravada Buddhism, in which he distinguishes two main categories of meditation: Samatha meditation and Vipassana meditation. According to Sumanasara, Samatha meditation is one in which the normal activity of the mind is suspended by focusing attention on an object, allowing the mind to unfold at a subtle level of activity. In Samatha meditation, by concentrating one's attention on a specific object, thoughts and their associated desires and emotions are suppressed, attachment to the object disappears, and one feels the joy of becoming one with the object itself at that moment. However, as one progresses through the stages, the state of zen meditation becomes more abstract and difficult to recognize and verbally express through consciousness.

Vipassana meditation, on the other hand, is a meditation technique that aims to observe things as they are and is what is called mindfulness meditation. Vipassana meditation is a continuous process of "bringing awareness and attention" to oneself and all that surrounds oneself and becoming aware of phenomena that come and go in the mind while also acting on one's own. A common exercise in mindfulness practice is to breathe in and out, keeping one's attention on all bodily movements that accompany the breath, as well as on the changes in the external world. This process is expected to inhibit the hijacking of attention to one part of the object, such as thoughts or actions, and to increase awareness, observation, and awareness of multiple phenomena, which in turn creates a state of mindfulness. Vipassana meditation is also said to promote trait change, or long-term change, and in this sense, the acquisition of a mindfulness attitude is thought to bring about long-term positive change.

4. Objectives of this study

4.1 Commonalities between mindfulness and PRIDE skills

Summarizing the core functions of mindfulness from the above points, (1) improvement of observation of oneself and others and (2) acquisition of attention control skills can be identified. The focus of this study began with the idea that there may be similarities between the acquisition of PRIDE skills in PCIT and the process of mindfulness attitude formation. In other words, in order to implement the verbal skills of "Labeled Praise," "Reflect," and "Behavior Descriptions" of the PRIDE skills, the skill user is conscious of and observes the various words and actions of the child (target) in the "here and now." Meanwhile, the skill user is required to switch his/her attention to himself/herself and immediately verbalize the skills. This is a very conscious internal process of verbalization. In other words, the skill user must continue to pay attention to multiple domains simultaneously, including the child's expressive behavior in the "here and now" and his or her own internal state. Such continuous use of the PRIDE skills is thought to enhance the skill user's ability to control attention and, as a result, contribute to the improvement of the observational function required for mindfulness. However, because PCIT uses the PRIDE skills in response to a child's good behavior, some may think that the added value judgment of good behavior is different from a mindfulness attitude. In reality, however, in PCIT, the caregiver (skill user) is always coached to emit the PRIDE skills for every behavior of the child, regardless of the outcome of the child's behavior (e.g., whether the child successfully piles blocks), except when the child is acting in a severely aggressive or destructive manner. As a result, in practical terms, the caregiver continually emits the PRIDE skills to the child at all times.

With the above as a research question, the present study will compare the changes in mindfulness scale scores of participants (skill users) before and after attending a 40-hour PCIT-International-approved PCIT Therapist Training Workshop (hereinafter referred to as "WS") to determine the potential of PCIT skill acquisition for the formation of mindfulness attitudes. Although this is a modest study, it is hoped that it will serve as one exploratory study to demonstrate the potential of PCIT as a behavioral guide for mindful parenting.

4.2 The three PRIDE skills and the hypothesis of this study

We will discuss in more detail the three PCIT skills that are the basis for the study and that are presumed to be related to mindfulness. Since three of the PRIDE skills, (1) Labeled Praise, (2) Reflect, and (3) Behavior Description, are the three verbal skills that are the criteria for CDI acquisition, the present study will focus on these three skills. Again, (1) Labeled Praise is a technique in which the skill user identifies and praises the child's specific behavior; (2) Reflect is a technique in which the skill user repeats the child's utterance verbatim, without changing the meaning; and (3) Behavior Descriptions is a technique in which the skill user describes the child's specific behavior in words, or in other words, a technique in which the skill user provides a live report of the situation.

In order to use the above three skills constantly, the skill user must be aware of the child's specific behavior and speech and must always pay attention to what the child says and does. Not only that, the skill user must also be careful not to use the Do not skills at the same time. In other words, the skill user must consciously select the appropriate skill and instantly verbalize it to the child so that the skill user does not utter "Question," "Command," or "Negative Talk." This is multitasking, and it occurred to me that this multiple and continuous attentional focus could produce the effects of attention control training and contribute to the improvement of observation and attention control skills, as referred to in mindfulness. In addition, mindfulness is not about concentrating on any one point but rather accepting and passing on internal and external stimuli that arise one after another. The state of mindfulness is created by not keeping awareness in one place but by quickly switching and dispersing attention to other areas to prevent "fixation" of awareness and to increase awareness with a broader perspective and distance. This process of mindfulness generation suggests that the use of the PRIDE skills is exactly in line with the mental state aimed for in Vipassana meditation, not Samatha meditation, and it is assumed that the use of the PRIDE skills has an element of mindfulness.

Approaching from the perspective of mindfulness meditation research, there have been many previous studies from the viewpoint that mindfulness meditation is involved in improving "attentional functions" [15]. Furthermore, Ogishima et al. [16] point out that attentional functions are categorized as subfunctions and that they may be associated with certain psychiatric disorders. Furthermore, Ogishima et al. [16] stated from their review of previous studies that it is unclear as to which attentional functions are associated with mindfulness meditation; however, they have consistently reported that there is an association between attentional functions and mindfulness. Ogishima et al. [16] categorized attentional functions into four subfunctions: "sustained attention," "selective attention," "executive attention," and "attention switching," and conducted a meta-analysis of the relationship between mindfulness meditation and attentional functions. The results showed that "sustained attention" had the greatest effect on mindfulness meditation. They also found that "executive function" had a moderate effect on mindfulness meditation, while "selective attention" and "attention switching" had a smaller effect on mindfulness meditation.

Next, we will consider the characteristics common to PRIDE skills in general for each of the four subfunctions of attention.

(1) "Sustained attention" is the continuous use of the attentional function, and in the PRIDE skills, the skill user's sustained focus of attention on the child is relevant. (2) "Selective attention" refers to the selection of the target of attention and may include the skill user selecting PRIDE skills that match the child's behavior and selectively suppressing the Do not skills. (3) "Executive attention" is an attentional function that sets a goal and regulates and inhibits one's own thoughts and feelings toward achieving the goal. This may also be applicable in that the skill user appropriately controls his/her own attention toward achieving the skill acquisition standard and executes verbalization of the skill. (4) "Attention switching" refers to redirecting attention from one object to another. Skill users emit appropriate skills one after another according to the ever-changing behavior of the children, and this may be a series of attention switching in which they alternately redirect their attention to the children's behavior and their own skills.

Thus, in PCIT, the skill user must constantly pay attention to the child while at the same time continuously redirecting attention to himself/herself and from there switch attention further to continue verbalizing his/her own skills. The purpose and hypothesis of this study is to investigate the possibility of improving mindfulness attitudes through the acquisition of PRIDE skills.

5. Method

5.1 Survey collaborators

For this study, I divided the participants into two groups: (1) the "PCIT skill acquisition group" (hereafter referred to as the "PCIT group") and (2) a control group (non-attendee group). The "PCIT group" was recruited from students attending a 5-day, 40-hour training workshop for PCIT therapists, following the PCIT-International prescribed curriculum and protocol (the training workshop was led by the author, a certified PCIT trainer). The manuals used in the WS were the PCIT Protocol 2011 Japanese version ver.2.0 (2013) and the DPICS, fourth Edition, Japanese ver.1.01 (2014), both prescribed by PCIT-International. The WS included the prescribed 13 lectures, skills role play, demonstration practice, and skills check.

In recruiting research collaborators, (1) the "PCIT group" were those who agreed to cooperate in the research after explaining the research to the students prior to the start of the course. All seven graduate students who took the course were selected as research collaborators because they all passed the final mastery check of PRIDE skills (mean age: 36.14 years; SD: 15.64). The "control group" consisted of six graduate students who had not taken the course and who had voluntarily applied for the recruitment of research collaborators at the college and who agreed to cooperate in the research after prior explanation (mean age: 22.67 years; SD: 0.51). The higher mean age of the PCIT group was due to the inclusion of one older student.

5.2 Measurement scale

The mindful attention awareness scale (MAAS) was used in this study as a measure of mindfulness characteristics. This is a mindfulness scale developed by Brown & Ryan [17], which was translated into Japanese and standardized by Fujino et al. [18]. According to the explanation by Fujino et al. [18], the foundations of mindfulness are awareness and attention. Awareness is the accompanying awareness of external and internal stimuli to the mind and body, which serves as a direct bridge between us and the events and experiences that surround us. Attention, on the other hand, is the focus of awareness on a particular stimulus, which increases our sensitivity to that stimulus. However, while people perceive stimuli, they are unable to keep their attention on the stimuli and are said to be mindless [17, 19]. The MAAS was developed to focus on this "awareness" and "attention" and is a one-factor, six-point, 15-item mindfulness measurement scale. Fujino et al. [18] conducted a detailed examination of the factor structure, internal consistency, and construct validity and concluded that the Japanese version of the MAAS measures the same characteristics as the original version and can be used to measure the relationship between mindfulness and well-being for a wide age group.

In addition, MAAS has the following characteristics. (1) Because the MAAS targets the degree of awareness and attention of adults in general who have no experience with meditation, it employs expressions that are rooted in daily life. In other words, the questionnaire items regarding mindless state were used because mindless state is generally easier to understand than mindful state, which the respondents had no experience with. (2) The MAAS measures the degree of the qualities of awareness and attention themselves, since it excludes questions on patience, trust, acceptance, calmness, and well-being, which are thought to result from the qualities of awareness and attention. (3) The MAAS distinguishes awareness and attention from reflexive consciousness, which is meta-consciousness, and targets the quality of awareness associated with the stimuli themselves before such judgments and evaluations of the self. (4) MAAS is negatively correlated with mind wandering and captures the "distraction of attention" itself. (5) Although the MAAS does not include direct well-being-related questions, it was found to be negatively correlated with negative well-being-related characteristic and positively correlated with positive well-being-related characteristics. (6) MAAS measures mindfulness as a trait but is also related to mindfulness as a state and to emotional state scales related to well-being. (7) MAAS scores are higher with mindfulness psychotherapy and are also associated with increased well-being, which is facilitated by mindfulness psychotherapy.

From these characteristics, it is understood that the MAAS is a measurement scale focusing on attentional functions, and therefore, I have adopted the MAAS as an appropriate scale for measuring mindfulness tendency in this study. Fujino et al. are experts in mindfulness meditation, and in preparing the Japanese version, they paid particular attention to the presence or absence of awareness and attention and were careful to ensure that the translation was faithful to the intent of the original version. Back-translation of the Japanese version of MAAS has confirmed that there are no differences in the Japanese-English wording. In standardizing the MAAS, Fujino et al. reversed the MAAS in order to see the relationship with other scales, but since the MAAS is originally composed of items focusing on the mindless state, it is judged that lower scores indicate a higher tendency toward mindfulness. Therefore, for the purposes of this paper, a higher MAAS score means a lower mindfulness tendency.

5.3 Survey period

For the "PCIT group," the survey was conducted over a longer period of time because the training course was divided into Part 1 and Part 2 instead of 5 consecutive days due to the graduate school curriculum (the WS was held in Part 1: July 13–15, 2019; Part 2: October 13–14 days). MAAS asked survey collaborators to conduct the survey before the start of the first session of WS and after the end of the last session. However, in order to maintain and improve their skills, the participants were required to practice PRIDE skills at least twice a week outside of the course days, at home for 5 minutes each time, targeting family members or videos of their children playing, and were asked to report their implementation to me immediately after each session via social networking. In addition, I asked all participants to report verbally on their skill practice during the interval period at the beginning of each course. In this way, I continued to reinforce the skills of the students. Three PRIDE skill-level checks were conducted on July 13, July 15, and October 14, and students were confirmed to be in

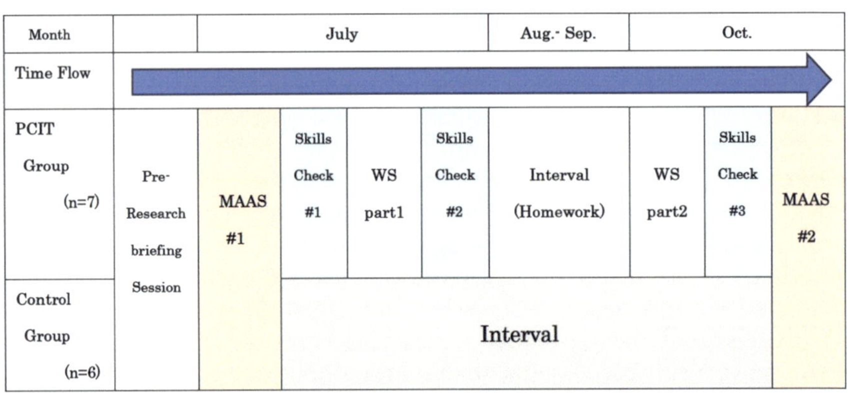

Figure 3.
Survey schedule. Note: The PCIT group was given the PRIDE skill check three times: immediately after the start of the WS, at the end of Part 1, and at the end of the WS. All participants reached mastery. Checks #1 and #3 were checked by coding on video, and a coding agreement rate of 70% or higher with the trainer each time was considered passing. Check #2 was conducted with a 5-minute role play by DPICS. A pass was determined when the skill use of the participant in the parent role reached the mastery criteria. The mastery criteria were the same as the normal PCIT criteria: Behavior Description, Labeled Praise, and Reflect each at least 10 times, and Question, Command, and Negative Talk no more than 3 times total.

satisfactory skill mastery status as of July 15 and October 14. The "control group" also performed two MAAS at the same interval as the PCIT group.

5.4 Method of implementation and ethical considerations

I explained to both the "PCIT group" and the "control group" the content of the survey and the ethical considerations before I began the study and had them sign a consent form. Subsequently, I administered the MAAS twice at the same interval to both groups at the beginning and end of the WS and obtained responses from all participants. This study was approved and conducted by the Ethics Committee of the Faculty of Human Sciences, Kobe College. There are no conflicts of interest. Survey participants were paid an honorarium after the second round of responses. The survey schedule is shown in **Figure 3**.

6. Results and discussion

6.1 Results of the survey

First, the Wilcoxon-signed rank test was used to compare the first MAAS scores between the PCIT and control groups, and no significant difference was found in the initial values between the two groups. Next, a Wilcoxon-signed rank test was conducted to compare the first and second MAAS scores of each group, and it was found that only in the PCIT group, $Z = -1.873$; there was a significant decreasing trend in MAAS, albeit at the 10% level (**Table 3**, **Figure 4**). In the control group, there was no significant difference between the first and second MAAS scores. Although the MAAS scores were apparently lower in the control group, this was due to outliers, and statistically, there was no change in mindfulness tendency in the control group. Since lower MAAS scores are associated with a higher tendency toward mindfulness, the MAAS scores of participants who mastered PCIT skills were confirmed to have decreased, albeit significantly. Thus, the results suggest that PCIT skill acquisition may increase mindfulness tendency.

In this study, I conducted a comparative study of mindfulness scores among PCIT WS participants and found that students in the PCIT group showed an increased tendency toward mindfulness even after attending only 5 days, conducted over a period of only 3 months. For the caregivers who receive PCIT, the PCIT sessions are basically conducted for 1 hour each week for about 20 sessions, so they will be learning PCIT skills for an even longer period of time (about 6 months) than the students in the current study. Thus, a caregiver who continuously learns the skills for a longer

	MAAS #1		MAAS #2			
	Mean	SD	Mean	SD	Z score	p
PCIT	50.57	13.7	47.29	12.6	−1.873	+
Control	48.17	15	43.33	11.3	−0.946	n.s.

$^{+}p < 0.1$.

Table 3.
Comparison of MAAS first and second scores.

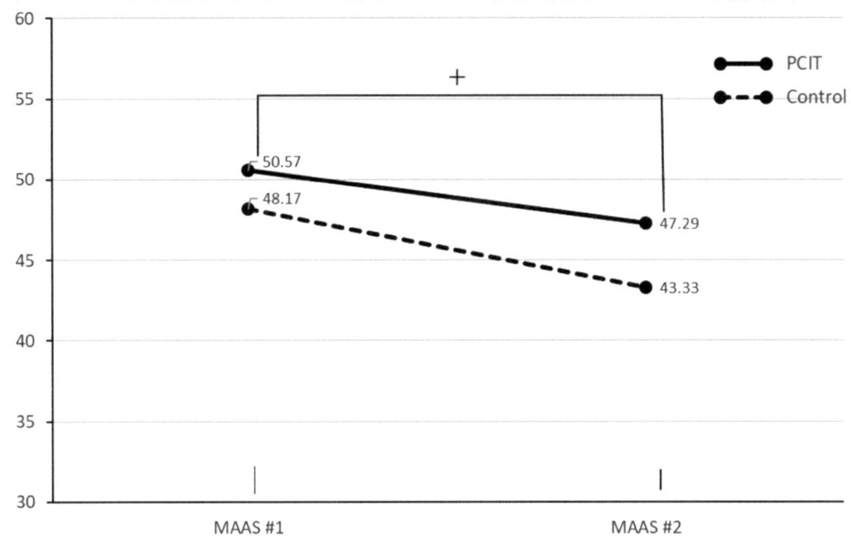

Figure 4.
Comparison of MAAS scores between the first and second MAAS.

period of time than the current student would have the experience to further train the "attention function" necessary to use the skill. It may be inferred from this result that caregivers, like the students, will have an increased attentional function and mindful attitude formation during the skill acquisition process. If caregivers can practice, learn, and use PRIDE skills on a daily basis, then PCIT can be said to provide a guide for caregivers to actually learn specific methodologies for "mindful parenting."

6.2 Limitations of this study

As I stated in the objectives, there are four subfunctions of attention that are important for mindfulness: sustained attention, selective attention, executive attention, and attention switching. A person who is trying to learn PCIT skills, in order to use the skills, keeps selective and sustained attention on the child (sustained attention), discards the appropriate skills (selective attention), takes action with a goal (executive attention), and instantly switches skills one after another according to the child's behavior (switching). If we may infer from this, we may assume that the attitude toward using PCIT skills is related to any of the attentional functions and that all of the attentional functions are essential to the improvement of PCIT skills. However, the present study could not clarify the mechanism of action of PCIT skills in relation to the subfunctions of attention and their effects on improving mindfulness attitudes. Although this was an exploratory study with a very small number of participants, this study may have opened the door for further research linking the effects of PCIT and mindfulness in the future. In order to further clarify these questions empirically in the future, it is necessary to increase the number of research collaborators and expand the scale of the study.

In addition, the research collaborators in this study were not actual child caregivers but rather graduate students who were studying to become PCIT therapists. In this regard, since the collaborators in this study had different motivations and backgrounds for learning PCIT than the caregivers, it is necessary to conduct a survey of caregivers during child-rearing in order to verify the actual "mindful parenting" effects of PCIT. These points are limitations of this study. However, when surveying PCIT caregivers, it takes time to conduct the cases themselves, and it is difficult to conduct a large number of cases at the same time; limitations exist due to the fact that PCIT is a psychotherapy. In order to conduct a large-scale study, it is necessary for multiple PCIT-implementing agencies to collaborate in planning, taking this into consideration. Research procedures would also benefit from an assessment of the personality of the skill users prior to skill acquisition. Qualitative studies such as interviews about mental processes in skill-use situations should be considered. In order to determine the direction of attention and the type of attention, it may be useful to confirm changes in the direction and duration of attention of skill users through the introduction of physiological devices such as an "eye tracker" that follows the viewpoint of the person using the skills. In mindfulness research, there are many studies using physiological measures such as EEG and fMRI during mindfulness. In the future, it will be necessary to construct more empirical research methods by physiologically measuring the state of mindfulness of skill users during PRIDE skill use.

Acknowledgements

This research was funded by a 2019 Kobe College of Human Sciences Educational Research Grant. I would also like to thank my research collaborators for their cooperation in this long-term study.

Author details

Tomoko Kuniyoshi
Department of Human Sciences, Kobe College, Nishinomiya, Hyogo, Japan

*Address all correspondence to: kuniyosi@mail.kobe-c.ac.jp

References

[1] Azhdari Z, Alizadeh M, Homaei R. The role of parent-child interaction therapy and mindfulness-based therapy on the behavioral problems of students with attention-deficit/hyperactivity disorder. International Journal of School Health. 2022;**9**(**1**):18-25 (Online article)

[2] Eyberg SM, Graham-Pole JR. Mindfulness and behavioral parent training: Commentary. Journal of Clinical Child & Adolescent Psychology. 2005;**34**(**4**):792-794

[3] Chaffin M, Silovsky JF, Funderburk B, Valle LA, Brestan EV, Balachova T, et al. Parent-child interaction therapy with physically abusive parents: Efficacy for reducing future abuse reports. Journal of Counseling and Clinical Psychology. 2004;**72**(**3**):500-510

[4] Eyberg S, Boggs SR, Algina J. Parent-child interaction therapy: Psychosocial model for the treatment of young children with conduct problem behavior and their families. Psychopharmacology Bulletin. 1995;**31**:83-91

[5] Thomas R, Abell B, Webb HJ, Avdagic E, Zimmer-Gembeck MJ. Parent-child interaction therapy: A meta-analysis. Pediatrics. 2017;**140**(3):e20170352. DOI: 10.1542/peds.2017-0352

[6] Thomas R, Zimmer-Gembeck MJ. Behavioral outcomes of parent–child interaction therapy and triple p-positive parenting program: A review and meta-analysis. Journal of Abnormal Child Psychotherapy. 2007;**35**(**3**):475-495

[7] Lieneman CC, Quetsch LB, Theodorou LL, Newton KA, McNeil CB. Reconceptualizing attrition in parent-child interaction therapy: "Dropouts" demonstrate impressive improvements. Psychology Research and Behavior Management. 2019;**12**:543-555

[8] Eyberg S, Funderburk BW. PCIT Protocol (Translated by Kamo T. (2013) PCIT Protocol, 2011, Japanese version 2.0.) Florida: PCIT International Inc; 2011

[9] Eyberg, S, Chase RM, et al. Dyadic Parent-Child Interaction Coding System (DPICS) Clinical Manual. 4th ed. (Translated by Kamo T. DPICS Manual version 4 (2014), Japanese Version 1.01). Florida: PCIT International Inc; 2014

[10] Kuniyoshi T. Consideration of the meaning of "Limit-Setting" in parent-child interaction therapy. Kobe College Studies. 2013;**60**(**1**):109-123 (Japanese)

[11] Kabat-Zinn J. Wherever You Go, There You Are: Mindfulness Meditation Everyday Life. New York: Hyperin; 1994

[12] Segal ZV, Williams JMG, Teasdale JD. Mindfulness-based Cognitive Therapy for Depression. The Guilford Press; 2002

[13] Gunaratana BH. Mindfulness in Plain English. Somerville: Wisdom Publications Inc.; 2011

[14] Sumanasara A. Meditation Methods for Modern People: Useful Early Buddhist Law. Vol. 4. Tokyo: Sanga; 2007

[15] Bishop SR, Shapiro LM, Carlson L, Anderson ND, Carmody J, Segal ZV, et al. Mindfulness: A proposed operational definition. Clinical Psychology: Science and Practice. 2004;**11**(**3**):230-241

[16] Ogishima H, Maeda S, Masuda Y, Shimada H. The effect of mindfulness mediation for attentional function:

A meta-analysis. Waseda Journal of Clinical Psychology. 2016;**16**(**1**):149-162 (Japanese)

[17] Brown KW, Ryan RM. The benefit of being present: Mindfulness and its role in psychological well-being. Journal of Personality and Social Psychology. 2003;**84**(**4**):822-848

[18] Fujino M, Kajimura S, Nomura M. Development and validation of the Japanese version of the mindful attention awareness scale using item response theory analysis. The Japanese Journal of Personality. 2015;**24**(**1**):61-76 (Japanese)

[19] Brown KW, Ryan RM, Creswell JD. Mindfulness: Theoretical foundations and evidence for its salutary effects. Psychological Inquiry. 2007;**18**:211-237

Chapter 5

Conflicts in PK-12 Schools: Causes, Consequences and Management

Parul Acharya

Abstract

This book chapter will focus on exploring the relationships between conflict management, communication, burnout, organizational support and effective strategies to cope with workplace stress in PK-12 school districts. The majority of work on conflict management focuses on corporations and for-profit organizations. However, teachers in PK-12 school districts are an important component of a country's workforce. This book chapter would discuss empirical research work that has examined these constructs from the teacher's perspective who are working in PK-12 school districts. Specifically, the relationships between conflict management, communication, burnout, organizational and coworker support will be examined. The strategies that teachers utilize to cope with stress and burnout will be discussed.

Keywords: PK-12 school teachers, conflict management, communication, stress and burnout, stress coping strategies, organizational, coworker support

1. Introduction

The majority of work on conflict management focuses on corporations and for-profit organizations. However, teachers in PK-12 school districts are an important component of a country's workforce. This chapter will focus on exploring empirical research on the relationships between conflict management, and the effective strategies to cope with workplace burnout and stress in teachers working within PK-12 school districts.

2. Causes of conflict in organizations

"Conflict is a type of behavior which occurs when two or more parties are in opposition or in battle as a result of a perceived relative deprivation from the activities of or interaction with another person or group" ([1], p. 180). It usually does not have a detrimental influence on the individuals when handled objectively and in a timely manner but it can lead to disruption in communication that impact the work efficiency when not addressed appropriately. There are several different causes of conflict. One of the most common causes of conflict is "means utilization." It is the situation where the disparate perspectives and viewpoints of how and who would utilize the resources leads to conflicts. Another common cause of conflict is "shared dependence on limited resources." In this situation, there are several agendas and priorities that are put forth by individuals and/or departments to obtain the resources. Shared dependence leads to competition for obtaining the most resources which eventually results in conflicts. "Scheduling problems is another source of conflict where new work norms and policies causes a disruption in existing standards and rules which may not be conducive and/or hard to adopt by employees (e.g., COVID-19 pandemic). It may lead to complaints, feeling of anxiety, stress, and resentment which are the main predecessors for burnout, mental health issues, and conflict [1]. Conflict can be social (disagreement with others in the workplace during public interactions), cognitive (emotional anxiety when person feels that their views are not acknowledged and valued and/or perceptions of unfair treatment), political (failure to reach consensus and form potential collaborations) or structural (ambiguity in job roles and responsibilities). The type of conflict and its source should be examined to explain the process of how the conflict started and proliferated in the workplace [2]. Conflicts can also exist in subsystems—"functional (e.g., competing priorities, incompatible job responsibilities-role conflict), social (feelings of anxiety, hostility, tension), informational (disagreement between parties and their choices), and political (inflexible demands by parties which inhibits formation of potential collaborations)" ([2], pp. 27–28).

3. Causes of conflicts in schools

Conflict is a common phenomenon that occurs in every organization including PK-12 schools. It may arise due to a variety of reasons which involves disagreement, and incompatibility between teacher-teacher, teacher-student, teacher-parent, and/or teacher-supervisor [3, 4], school climate [5], and other individual and contextual-level factors [6–12]. The most common sources of conflict in PK-12 schools are the distribution of work load and resources, teacher-student relationship, teacher-parent interaction, classroom management, teaching methods, assessment practices, role conflict where the jobs responsibilities are not clearly delineated, power struggle with coworkers and superiors, individual attitudes, and political issues [13–15]. Conflicts leads to disruption or cessation of individual, interpersonal and organizational work activities which negatively influences the productivity at micro and macro level of school environment. Conflicts are inevitable in schools as there is constant interaction between teachers, students, parents, and administration. Hence, it is essential to comprehend the root cause and dynamics of conflict in an appropriate and timely manner which would help to mitigate the negative results in schools and also to establish benchmarks to improve school's effectiveness [16–19].

4. Consequences of conflicts in schools

The study conducted by Ertürk [20] provided the positive and negative results of conflicts. The most common negative effects of conflict at the individual-level are "weariness, fatigue, burnout, reluctance to do work, reduced productivity and performance, decreased organizational commitment, stress and fatigue." The common interpersonal effects of conflict are "difficulty in communication, unwillingness to collaborate and share, and reluctance to talk." The negative results of conflict at the organizational level are increase in "negative and unproductive behaviors at workplace, formation of groups based on pessimistic ideologies, deterioration of school climate, and decrease in collaboration and teamwork" (p. 258). The positive consequences of conflict at the individual-level are "increase in productivity, resolution of misunderstandings, acknowledging different views, and learning from others". At the organizational-level, the results could be "development of new ideas and leadership role, and increase in the democratic process" (p. 259). The most common consequences of conflict are "weariness and fatigue, burnout, reluctance to do work, reduced productivity and performance, decreased organizational commitment, stress and anxiety, isolation, unhappiness, cynicism, decrease in motivation, reluctance to come to the school, desire to get away from the school, ethical behaviors' starting to disappear, retreat and anger are the individual negative effects of conflicts" ([20], p. 263). Role conflict and role ambiguity are the two aspects of role stress which is commonly encountered by teachers. Role conflict occurs when the job responsibilities are convoluted and a discrepancy exists between the expectations and employee perspective. Role ambiguity occurs when there is scarce (inadequate and incomplete) availability of accurate information that is needed to effectively accomplish the assigned work responsibilities.

This section would focus primarily on teacher burnout and stress as these are the most commonly encountered consequences of conflict that has been widely examined in the empirical research literature. "Burnout is the combination of the inability and unwillingness to spend the necessary effort at work for proper task completion" [21]. It causes emotional fatigue, depersonalization and lack of personal achievement [22] Burnout is expressed through three dimensions-exhaustion, cynicism, and lack of professional efficacy [23]. Burnout and stress have been attributed to high teacher attrition in school district. Hence, it is important to review empirical research and the role of constructs that influence teacher burnout and stress to comprehend the context and sources of conflict that occur in schools. There are a few review studies that were conducted on burnout in special education teachers [24–28]. The synthesis of Brunsting et al. [24] reviewed research articles on teacher burnout from 1979 to 2013. The study showed that emotional regulation and stress management were the key constructs that reduced burnout. The school-level factors of role conflict, role ambiguity, and support from the administration were also predictive of teacher burnout. Park and Shin [26] divided burnout into three domains-emotional exhaustion, depersonalization, and personal accomplishment. The influence of student (e.g., behavior problems, class size, socio-economic status), teacher (demographics, self-efficacy, stress coping strategies), and school related variables (workplace obstacles, support from leadership and coworkers, emotional experience in workplace, availability of resources) on the three domains were assessed separately. The protective effects of self-efficacy, personal accomplishment, job satisfaction (teacher-level variables) from emotional exhaustion was consistently seen in all the reviewed studies. Depersonalization was greater when there were higher levels of coping, self-efficacy and teaching experience. In terms of school-related variables, a higher level of support from school personnel and emotional experience led to higher levels of personal accomplishment. These school-level variables also had protective effects from emotional exhaustion, and burnout. An increase in workplace obstacles led to greater depersonalization.

The review by Wisniewski and Gargiulo [27] examined mediating variables that influenced teacher burnout. The results showed that clarity in the communication of roles and responsibilities reduced burnout. Furthermore, interactions with coworkers and other school personnel and stress conditions in classrooms (student's behavioral and emotional issues) impacted burnout in teachers. A literature review was conducted by Konukman et al. [10] on teachers who had both coaching and instructional responsibilities. The review explored the influence of role conflict on burnout and stress in physical education teachers. The study showed that the dual responsibilities of teaching and coaching in terms of time requirements, instructional needs, and motivation are important factors that impact burnout and stress in physical education teachers. A systematic review was conducted by Nwoko et al. [29] in which four factors influenced teacher's occupational well-being and helped them to manage conflicts. These factors were (1) personal teacher capabilities (resilience, self-efficacy, autonomy, and coping strategies); (2) socio-emotional intelligence (emotional competence, training opportunities, and other supportive work relationships); (3) personal responses (workload and work conditions included burnout, fatigue, exhaustion, stress, unrealistic expectations, stress, bureaucracy, and exclusion from decisions); (4) relational factors (student misconduct, misunderstandings with parents and coworkers, and perceived lack of support from the school management system)" (pp. 11–12).

The systematic review conducted by Mijakoski et al. [30] explored the determinants of burnout in longitudinal studies. The quantitative synthesis mainly revolved around emotional exhaustion that occurred due to burnout. There were four primary determinants identified in the study that were categorized to have either a detrimental or protective effect from conflicts. These four determinants were "conflicts with coworkers, emotional strain, parent criticism, and obstacles from parents or students" (p. 5). Conflict arising from any source had a negative relationship with emotional exhaustion. Conflicts can be managed through any type of help or endorsement in the form of assistance through resources, information and/or emotion received from coworkers, supervisor or organization, and community. The presence of social integration, social support, and high-quality relationships in the workplace has a protective effect from conflicts. Another important source of conflicts can also arise from individual characteristics that consists of emotional dissonance, depersonalization, cynicism, teacher's self-efficacy in student behavior management, neuroticism (negative feelings, such as anxiety, anger, depression, frustration), and job satisfaction. Teacher self-efficacy and job satisfaction had a negative relationship with conflict. Organizational context also has an important role to play in conflict. It comprises of "time pressure, classroom disruption, perceived collective exhaustion, perceived collective cynicism, workload stressors, technical obstacles, effective class management, work climate (pressure), supportive school climate, and collective teacher efficacy" (p. 5). Overall, the systematic review of studies showed that the quality of relationships in the workplace, social integration, individual-level behavioral traits, and organizational context (climate) influenced the nature and intensity of conflicts which can lead to stress and burnout in teachers.

The empirical literature on teacher stress and burnout that can arise due to conflicts at workplace discusses the role of fairness and organizational justice. It is the extent to which employees feel that they are fairly treated at their workplace. According to Colquitt [31], workplace justice is perceived based on the fair allocation of resources (distributive justice), procedures used to make decisions usually related to hiring, promotion, pay/benefits (procedural justice), treatment from coworkers and superiors (interactional justice), and information shared within the organization (informational justice). Conflicts arises when teachers see a mismatch between the resources, decisions, treatment, and/or information they receive from the school administration. This discrepancy between teacher expectations (what they deserve) and the actual outcome (what they receive) raises stress and burnout due to the conflicts. Adeyemi [32] showed that insufficient resources and facilities for teachers and students can be a source of conflicts which negatively influenced academic achievement. Ozgan [33] conducted a study to investigate the strategies of conflict management in the context of fairness in schools, teacher's commitment and confidence and their evaluation of school administrator or principal. The results showed that teacher's who had higher perceived scores on organizational justice, strategies of conflict management, and commitment, had greater level of confidence and gave higher evaluation scores to the school principal. Hoy and Tarter [4] demonstrated that "principal is the single most important person in developing a sense of organizational justice in school. The principal of the school is much more important than the faculty in creating a just and fair school at least with respect to professional interactions" (p. 257). The authors also noted that trust in the coworkers is also an important factor to develop perceptions of workplace fairness. Sehgal and Verma [34] showed that the three forms of justice (interactional, procedural, and distributive) is positively correlated with organizational commitment and negatively correlated with occupational stress. Social exchange theory explains that effort directed in the workplace is closely tied to the expected rewards. So, fairness perceptions of the rewards received based on the effort exerted by an employee acts as a protective buffer from conflicts, stress and burnout [35]. Several other studies demonstrate the positive relationships between organizational justice. Job satisfaction, school climate [36], and commitment [37]. Capone and Petrillo [36] developed a self-report questionnaire of organizational justice index to measure perceptions of teacher fairness. The questionnaire can be used to evaluate the organization issues that lead to feelings of unfairness by teachers and to develop relevant interventions and strategies to fix the issues related to organizational problems that lead to perception of unfairness in the workplace. Organizational fairness has negative associations with burnout (emotional exhaustion, depersonalization and lack of personal accomplishment—[38]), stress [39].

5. School climate and conflict management

The literature on conflicts in school districts have explored the role of school climate or school culture in the form of support provided to teachers from principals, colleagues, and resources to manage conflicts and stress. School climate has been defined in several different ways in the research literature. In general, school climate refers to the "quality and characteristics of school life, based on the patterns people experience in that life, and it reflects standards, goals, values, interpersonal relationships, the practice of teaching and learning, and the structure of the organization [40]". The various aspects of school climate include (but not limited to) work responsibilities, assessment and teaching practices, teacher-student and teacher-parent relationships (pupil discipline), teacher interactions with coworkers, superiors, and stakeholders, mentoring and induction programs [41], workplace well-being, job satisfaction, and stress [7–9, 11, 12, 42]. Otrebski [43] showed that teacher's perceptions of organizational climate can strongly influence their job satisfaction as well as positive (enthusiasm and effort) and negative (anxiety and depression) emotions. A positive perception of school climate enhances the feeling of job satisfaction and positive emotions. School climate has been shown to influence teacher's work commitment, job satisfaction, resilience, and their mental health, well-being and stress [44] which play an important role in conflict management. On the reverse side, teacher's stress also influences classroom climate as shown by a correlational study which investigated the role of teacher's stress states on classroom cohesion, flexibility and communication (three aspects of classroom climate). Sönmez and Kolaşınlı [45] showed that teacher's stress negatively influenced the flexibility (absence of free learning environment) and communication dimension (limited student-teacher interaction). Lambert et al. [46] identified teacher, classroom/school and state-level variables that predicted teacher's risk for occupational stress and burnout. The classroom/school-level variables were number of struggling students (higher number showed more stress), and school location (teachers working in Title I, urban and rural schools had higher stress than suburban). The teacher-level variables were years of experience (more experience had lower stress), subject area specialist or special education teacher (higher stress). The state-level variables related to policy climate, such as states with higher standards for assessment and accountability led to a higher stress score.

A study conducted by Nalipay [47] examined the influence of school-level indicators of climate (academic pressure, engagement of stakeholders, availability of special needs personnel, school delinquency and violence) and teacher-level indicators (disciplinary climate, teacher-student relations, and stakeholder participation) on teacher job satisfaction, workplace well-being and stress (dependent variables). The results of multi-level analyses showed that the dependent variables were more influenced by teacher related indicators than school-level measures. All the teacher-level indicators had a significant influence on job satisfaction. In general, school-level indicators did not have a significant predictive ability on the dependent variable. Workplace well-being and stress were positively influenced by disciplinary climate but negatively influenced by stakeholder's participation. These results indicate that individual-level characteristics are a stronger determinant of job satisfaction, workplace well-being and stress. Another study investigated the role of school climate factors (e.g., affiliation, student support and conduct, innovation, resource adequacy, work pressure, staff freedom and self-governance) on teacher self-efficacy and stress. The school-level factors which reduced stress were student conduct and staff autonomy whereas work pressure increased stress. Affiliation, professional interest, and innovation had a positive impact on teacher's self-efficacy. Teacher's stress was not found to be a mediator when examining the relation between school climate and teacher self-efficacy [48]. The mediating role of teacher's self-efficacy in explaining school climate (collegial leadership and teacher professionalism) and stress is explained in Hu et al. [49] study. The study results showed that both leadership and professionalism had a statistically significant negative impact on teacher stress through self-efficacy. In other words, teachers who had self-efficacy reported a more positive outlook of leadership and professionalism due to which had perceived lower stress levels. The research on school climate in the context of conflict management and teacher's stress has also examined the role of inclusive education practices that have the potential to impact teacher well-being, student achievement and parent's experiences [44]. In this study, the contribution of stressors, risk and protective factors, and inclusive practices on teacher well-being were examined. The well-being of employees and the implementation of inclusive practices (training for content readiness, manage increase workload and handle students with diverse learning needs) reduces the chance of conflicts, stress and burnout.

The school climate has also been examined in the context of cognitive behavioral therapy and tension regulation strategies (e.g., emotional regulation, cognitive reappraisal methods, suppression and resilience) that teachers use for stress management [50, 51]. A study conducted by Jeon and Ardeleanu [52] investigated teacher perceptions of work climate (work situations), family support, children's behaviors, and perceived stress measured through use of strategies to control their emotions. This study utilized stress coping methods that teachers utilize when dealing with external stressors which can come from either the environment or from individuals or both. Path analysis results show that reappraisal coping strategy acted as a mediator to explain the relationship between work situation and teacher stress. In other words, teacher's experienced less stress when they used reappraisal as a stress coping strategy to deal with work situations. Suppression was the mediator between children's behaviors and stress. This indicates that teacher's experienced less stress when they used suppression as a coping method to manage children's behaviors (or classroom management). Covariates, such as teacher's age (older) and general health (poor health) also predicted higher stress levels. Blacks, and non-Hispanic teachers used reappraisal for emotional regulation better than White, non-Hispanic teachers. Teachers who had a bachelor's degree and had higher household income reported to utilize less suppression as an emotional regulator. Teacher resilience has been investigated in the form of emotional (self-care), professional (competence), motivational (self-efficacy) and social (relationships) to see its impact on conflict and stress management. A literature review on teacher resilience showed that personal-level variables such as moral values, persistence, self-efficacy, coping skills (emotional regulation), teaching skills, professional growth and reflection were important for the management of stress and conflicts. The contextual-level variables included support from school administration (e.g., constructive feedback), mentors and coworkers, student relationships, training received during pre-service years and family support [53]. The specific strategies identified in this literature review to increase teacher well-being and decrease conflicts through the practice of resilience were the involvement in collaborative work activities with coworkers and superiors, to build positive relationships in the workplace (including with students and their parents), segregate work from home to avoid personal conflicts due to professional pressure at workplace (or vice-versa), participation in professional development activities, fair distribution of responsibilities, establishment of clear behavioral expectations and student engagement in classroom to build a healthy environment.

School principals and administrators have a pivotal role to play in conflict management and resolution [42]. There is research on the role of school leadership support (principal's collegial and supportive behavior, school management, instructional leadership), and contextual factors (school climate and structure, academic expectations, justness and fairness in policies, support and resources) to explain conflicts, stress and coping in teachers [54–59]. Berkovich and Eyal [60] reported that school principals can provide emotional support to teachers through a less formalized work environment, supportive and engaging work climate, common goals, professional knowledge, and perceived accessibility (quality of relationship-transparency and trust; demographic similarity-age and gender). Herman et al. [61] conducted a study where the principals took leadership training program in behavior support. The teachers of these schools were found to be more adaptive (low stress and high coping skills) than schools were the principals did not go through the program (teachers were normative-high stress and less coping). A meta-analysis study on leadership, role ambiguity, conflicts, and structure indicated that extensive workload, interpersonal conflicts, and deficiency of organizational fairness are the most important contributors of teacher stress [62]. The social support from principal and colleagues can fulfill teacher's basic needs for autonomy, competence and relatedness and reduce the effects of time pressure, and unclear organizational conditions [63]. Job demands and job resource mediated the relationship between social support received from principal and basic needs. Similar results are seen for unclear organizational conditions as a mediator between principal's social support and the three basic teacher needs. These results indicate that social support from principals influences the job demands and resources because they can remove the ambiguity and conflict present in teacher roles and responsibilities through clear communication, fair accountability practices, and positive work climate. This in turn, fulfills teacher's basic needs and reduces the likelihood of conflicts. Time pressure has a negative impact on both autonomy and competence dimensions of basic needs. Social support from colleagues mediated the relationship between principal support and relatedness and autonomy [63]. A research study investigated the association between organizational performance, principal's management skills to resolve the conflicts between teacher-teacher, teacher-student, and parent-teacher. The correlation analysis showed that principal's management skills to resolve conflict had a significant relationship with organizational performance and teacher-teacher, teacher-student, and parent-teacher conflict and organizational performance. This study highlights the importance of principal's ability to effectively resolve conflicts which if not addressed in a timely and appropriate manner can lead to hostility, stress, burnout, and reduction in work performance [64]. Fabunimi and Alimba [3] supported the results of this study and indicated that principal's inability to manage disputes is the major source of conflicts in secondary schools.

A study conducted by Rave et al. [65] showed that organizational citizenship behavior (OCB) of teachers as a group is influenced by the extent to which the school principal attentively listen to their teachers. In this study, teacher's perception of their principal's listening quality was used to measure the support the principal had towards teachers. The results showed a positive relationship between perceived principal's listening quality and group OCB and a negative relationship with teacher's turnover intentions. The interaction between listening and teacher stress significantly predicted turnover intentions. Specifically, the perceived listing quality of principals was related to a greater reduction in teacher turnover intentions who reported moderate to high stress levels. This means that better is the perceived listening quality of principals, lower is the turnover intentions of teachers who had moderate and high stress. Listening quality of principals also led to higher group OCB in teachers. A systematic review synthesized the research literature on stress, job satisfaction, burnout and turnover intentions in secondary general education teachers [66]. In terms of job satisfaction, the results showed that teachers who worked in smaller schools and in small towns had higher levels of job satisfaction than teachers working in larger and rural schools. The independence teachers have in their jobs, relationships, with students, connection with their schools, and self-efficacy had a positive impact on their job satisfaction. The major school-level stress factors were limited support from the administration, inconducive school climate, lack of adequate training on classroom and workload management. The accountability policies imposed by state and federal legislation (e.g., No Child Left Behind, Every Student Success Achievement Act, Race to the Top) led to decrease in teacher autonomy over curriculum which resulted in depersonalized teaching, dissatisfaction with the polices, and increase in stress levels and turnover intentions.

Teacher's social identity has been researched in the context of school climate and stress over time by Willis et al. [67]. The data was collected in two waves. Social identification was a mediator between school climate and stress which were measured in wave 1 and 2 respectively. The results of structural equation model show that a more positive teacher perception of school climate and social identification at wave 1 led to a higher score on their self-esteem over time at wave 2. School climate shared a significant relationship with social identification. The mediating effect of social identification on the relationship between school climate and self-esteem was also significant. The literature on social roles explain the importance of identity in the workplace. Identity is an individual's perception of self-concept based on their competence, beliefs, motivation, personality, mindset and values. Identity helps the individual to define their position in a professional or personal role [68]. Social identification is important because it is an important determinant of group membership, and self-esteem. Teachers perceive themselves based on the nature of their communication and interaction within their workplace [69]. A longitudinal study on teacher's professional identity showed that a balance between the three work dimensions (personal-time with family and for leisure; professional-roles and responsibilities; and situational-context of work environment) had a positive influence on their job satisfaction and psychological well-being [70]. A study conducted by Padmanabhanunni and Pretorius [71] showed that teacher's identity was negative correlated with anxiety, hopelessness, role ambiguity, and role stress. In other words, teacher's who had a higher perception of their identity as an educator had levels of ambiguity, anxiety and stress. A longitudinal study examined teacher's perceived stress levels (time 3) through coworker support (time 2) and cooperation frequency (time 1) for class preparation [72]. A hierarchical model was implemented to analyze the influence of between-group variable, group-level (school) on within-group, individual-level variables (colleague support and cooperation frequency). The results showed a statistically significant influence of cooperation frequency on teacher's stress at the within-group level but not at the between-group level when mediated by colleague's support. These results show that teachers who prepared for classes with colleagues at time 1 reported lower workplace stress at time 3 than teachers who worked by themselves to prepare for classes. Furthermore, greater colleague support was reported at time 2 by those teachers who had worked with other teacher on class preparation in time 1. This study highlights the role of coworker cooperation in encouraging teachers to participate in job-related professional development and the importance of collective effort for class preparation that helps to enhance instructional quality and reduce teacher stress.

On similar lines, organizational and social support (in the form of interactions with coworkers and superiors) have protective effects from occupational stressors (Climate and Organizational Functioning; Pressure at Work; Infrastructure and Routine work activities), and burnout (Emotional exhaustion/Professional frustration and Depersonalization/Detachment) as shown in the study conducted by Baptista and Cardoso [73]. The study highlights that low quality of affective relationships with coworkers, limited relationships with superiors, less opportunities for professional development and growth, insufficient bonuses, limited communication, and inadequate acknowledgement and appreciation at the workplace can increase stress and burnout in teachers. The role of mentoring support in reducing risk of stress in teachers has also shown to reduce the risk of conflicts, occupational stress and burnout in teachers. Boyle et al. [74] showed that teachers who were assigned a mentor at the workplace experiences less stress risk than teachers who were not allocated a mentor. The literature on mentoring support provides evidence of the benefits teachers receive from mentors assigned to them in schools. The study conducted by Kapadia et al. [75] highlights the advantages of mentoring program for novice teachers (beginning career) in the form of teaching strategies, classroom management and observation, and the supportive role of school principals. On similar lines, Ronfeldt and McQueen [76] analyzed data from US National Center for Education Statistics (NCES) to demonstrate that an assigned mentor during the first-year of teaching significantly reduced the odds of turnover intentions in teachers. The research on mentoring also provides evidence of induction programs that school districts should have which has a positive impact on occupational commitment, job satisfaction, teacher retention, pedagogical methods and practices, and student achievement with decrease in turnover intentions [41]. The research studies on teacher mentoring and induction programs highlights the need of such initiatives by school district administration to address the antecedents (e.g., support and resources on teaching, classroom management, lesson planning, assessments, student-teacher relationships, parent-teacher relationships) that can lead to conflicts, stress and burnout in teachers.

6. Teacher self-efficacy and conflict management

This section reviews the research literature on the role of self-efficacy as an important coping strategy to manage conflicts, stress and burnout in teachers [77–80]. In the previous section, we saw that school climate plays an important role in teacher's self-efficacy. Self-efficacy is the extent to which an individual feels competent and confident to efficiently complete the assigned responsibilities, resolve conflicts, and manage stress. A study conducted by Betoret and Artiga [81] showed that self-efficacy (teacher's ability to efficiently implement the teaching process and classroom management) along with active coping strategy provides a protective effect against pedagogical barriers (stressors) at the classroom-level (workload, student misbehavior and demotivation, and student diversity), school-level (lack of decision-making, and ambiguity in administrative demands), parent's level (passive parental involvement) and on burnout (emotional exhaustion, low personal accomplishment and depersonalization-dependent variables). The hierarchical regression results show that majority of pedagogical barriers increase emotional exhaustion, and makes the teachers feel low about their personal achievement and depersonalization. All student-level (except student diversity) factors increase the scores of the three dependent variables related to burnout. The school-level (except ambiguity in demands), and parent-level factor also had enhanced the negative feelings of burnout in teachers. Active coping (ability to deal with the problems directly) reduced the three indicators of burnout while passive coping (avoidance of direct conflict with problems) increased burnout. The self-efficacy in teachers decreased with increase in work experience and that primary school teachers reported higher efficacy scores than secondary school teachers. Self-efficacy had a negative impact on passive coping. Self-efficacy on instructional management had a positive impact on active coping strategy. These results indicate that teachers who have higher efficacy have the ability to directly deal with the problem at hand rather than avoiding it to reduce stress. A similar study showed that self-efficacy mediated the effect of perceived stress and job burnout (emotional exhaustion, depersonalization, and reduced accomplishment). In other words, self-efficacy helps teachers to develop effective strategies to deal with job-related stressors and helps them to develop a positive attitude and mindset towards teaching. The development of a positive mindset helps the teachers to perceive their failures as opportunities for learning and for regulation their emotions [82]. Putwain and von der Embse [83] showed that perceived self-efficacy of teachers moderated the relationship between pressure arising from curriculum changes and perceived stress. In other words, teachers who had higher self-efficacy scores had lower perceived stress when compared to teachers who reported lower self-efficacy. Another study reported that self-efficacy fully mediated the relationship between social support at workplace and teacher's job satisfaction. The study also revealed that the likelihood of teachers to give positive reviews about the school administration was higher when they received frequent and immediate feedback from the school's leadership [84].

Jeon et al. [85] examined the role of three types of self-efficacy (general teaching efficacy, personal teaching efficacy, and disciplinary teaching efficacy) on teachers' self-perceived psychological well-being, stress, and emotional exhaustion. General teaching efficacy had a negative association with stress and emotional exhaustion indicating that teachers who have confidence in their teaching had lower feelings of stress and emotional fatigue. Disciplinary teaching efficacy had a negative impact on emotional exhaustion. This result shows that teachers have lower emotional exhaustion when they have higher levels of efficacy to discipline children. The study results also showed that teachers had lower levels of depressive symptoms, stress and emotional exhaustion when they have positive perceptions of their work environment (professional development opportunities, family support, less chaos in child care at school and children's behavior). Self-efficacy has also been investigated in consonance with teacher resilience which is an important strategy for emotional regulation (ability to effectively manage one's emotions due to job-related stress). Li [86] showed that teacher's self-efficacy and emotional regulation had a positive impact on their resilience. Teacher self-efficacy had a protective effect from teacher burnout. The results further showed that resilience fully mediated the relationship between teacher self-efficacy and burnout. The study shows that teachers who have higher self-efficacy in their teaching competence are more resilient, tend to spend more time and effort to be engaged in their responsibilities, have a higher sense of belonginess to the school, and experience less burnout. Klassen et al. [87] showed that self-efficacy mediated the relationship between job stress from student's behavior in teachers across three different countries (Canada, England and Thailand). In other words, teachers who had self-efficacy were better able to handle student's behavior and deal with their job-related stress.

The longitudinal impact of self-efficacy (school and class) and induction program on beginning teacher's (3 years' experience) psychological well-being (perceived discontentment and job tension) was examined in an experimental study. The teachers in experimental group schools had developed and implemented an induction program whereas control group teachers had no such program. The results showed that over time, higher is teacher's perceived self-efficacy, lower is their discontentment and job tension. On the other hand, higher is the perceived stress over time, higher would be the perceived discontentment and job tension. The comparison between experimental and non-experimental school shows that an increase in the school self-efficacy scores of teachers in the induction program causes a reduction in job tension 10 times more when compared to teachers who were not in any induction program. An increase in class self-efficacy scores of teachers in the induction program leads to a decrease in job discontentment scores that is 16 times stronger when compared to teachers in the control group. School self-efficacy had an eight times lower influence on job discontentment for control group teachers when compared to experimental group teachers. In both groups, higher self-efficacy lead to lower job discontentment [88]. A mixed-methods study investigated the influence of online professional development program on teacher's self-efficacy, burnout and stress. The study was an experimental study in which teachers were randomly assigned into three different treatment groups (course-only, coaching, and reflective writing) and one control group. No significant differences were found between the experimental groups with regards to changes in stress, self-efficacy, emotional exhaustion, and personal accomplishment when compared to the control group. No significant differences were found in self-efficacy among the coaching and reflective writing group when compared to control group. The course-only group had lower self-efficacy scores in comparison to control group. The qualitative results showed that coaching and reflective writing groups helped teachers to express their emotions when they were exhausted and had low levels of self-efficacy. Course-only teachers became more emotionally worn-out and showed lower self-efficacy than reflective writing group. Teachers in coaching group were able to talk about the challenges and obtain quick feedback which helped them to cope up with emotional exhaustion and lower self-efficacy [89].

7. Interventions for stress management

The immediate consequence of workplace conflicts is stress. The empirical literature on teacher stress management have investigated the use of different type of techniques, such as knowledge-based (teacher education on problem behaviors), behavioral (meditation and relaxation), and cognitive-behavioral interventions (social-emotional learning, manual based treatment protocol, stress management approaches) as well as mindfulness training [90] that helps to manage stress [91]. Mindfulness is defined as the purposeful experience of the present moment without making any judgments or decisions about it. The self-awareness, regulation and transcendence framework explain that the practice of mindfulness can help the individual to separate their feelings and thoughts from circumstance and/or people causing conflicts in workplace which helps to reduce stress and burnout [92]. The literature reports five dimensions of mindfulness which are acting with awareness, describing, observing/ noticing, nonreactivity to inner experience, and nonjudging of inner experience [93]. A study conducted by Aundrea and Bostain [94] showed than teacher's mindfulness had positive relationships with their resilience to manage burnout. A review of literature on mindfulness interventions for teachers shows its beneficial effects in the form of reduction in depression, anxiety, and tension and an increase in attention, memory capacity, and adaptability to manage work tension [90]. The results of a randomized controlled trial showed the effects of an intervention that combined mindfulness and social-emotional learning. The intervention significantly reduced perceived stress in secondary teachers and conflict in student-teacher relationship [95]. These studies highlight the importance of behavioral, cognitive and mindfulness interventions to manage conflicts in school environment and reduce stress and burnout in teachers.

8. Teacher conflict and stress during COVID-19

The pandemic brought unrealistic and unexpected changes in the school's work environment where all classroom teaching and other activities shifted to completely online mode. These sudden changes led to increase in teacher anxiety, stress and burnout due to role ambiguity, role conflict and minimal support from the school district administration [62, 96–98], and psychosomatic health problems due to psychosocial demand factors (job insecurity, workload, lack of organizational justice) and lack of social support [99]. Teacher's had to manage conflicts and stress arising from environmental, (school administration, student's home environment and parent-teacher relationship), role related (climate and classroom management, virtual teaching, and student issues), and personal factors (work-family balance, uncertainty and work over load) as reported in a study by Boneh et al. [100]. Teacher's mental health was also impacted during COVID-19 as examined in a systematic review conducted by Santiago et al. [101]. The review showed that generalized anxiety disorders were associated with several risk factors, such as age (younger individuals), gender (females), ethnicity (African-American/Black), low income, having own children, and lower job stability with less than 5 years teaching experience. Burnout syndrome was associated with teacher's emotional exhaustion, depression (due to work-family conflict, work stress, limited social and emotional support, alteration in the social relationships in workplace, job instability and job loss) and depersonalization as well as lack of professional accomplishment. This syndrome was reported more in special education teachers. Technostress ("unsuccessful adaptation due to failure in dealing with technology and changes in the requirements related to the use of technology" p. 24) was also a major cause of burnout. The review indicated that resilience, and job satisfaction were commonly found to cope with anxiety, burnout, and stress [102]. The antecedents of burnout during COVID-19 were gender, age, perceived vulnerability to disease, perceived infectability, germ aversion, and role stress (role ambiguity and role conflict). The dimensions of burnout were anxiety, depression, hopelessness, and dissatisfaction with life. Emotional exhaustion, depersonalization, and personal accomplishment explained psychological well-being. Results showed that women reported higher emotional exhaustion. All the dimensions of burnout significantly predicted the constructs that explained psychological well-being. Fear of COVID-19, role ambiguity and role conflict were significant predictors of burnout [103].

9. Teacher coping and conflict management during COVID-19

Teachers were faced to enhance their cognitive and emotional coping skills to deal with the pedagogical challenges and conflicts to reduce the intensity of stress and burnout during COVID-19. The presence of social support from coworkers and school administration, coping resources helps the employee to meet the workplace demands and also have flexibility to the change or shift in job responsibilities [104, 105]. Teachers had to develop new plans for instruction, classroom management, student engagement and assessment. The disruption in routine procedures and increase in work load also meant that it was important to review research on conflict management strategies to reduce burnout and stress. The study conducted by Truzoli et al. [106] showed that teacher's self-efficacy, locus of control and stress coping strategies (planning class activities, comparing oneself with coworkers, confiding in family and friend, finding alternative means for relaxation) had protective effects on anxiety, stress, and aggression). The study also showed that teacher's technological skills, support received from school, satisfaction with online teaching, and appropriate communication in online teaching were reported to be effective coping strategies to manage anxiety and stress.

A mixed-methods study conducted by Hidalgo-Andrade et al. [107] concluded that social support (family, friends, spiritual activities) was the most frequently used coping strategy during the pandemic to manage psychological distress followed by leisure activities, mental health promotion (psychological well-being), and work with study (professional growth). Another study conducted by Porru et al. [108] assessed teacher's perception of risk to contract COVID and the effectiveness of health measures (EHM). The risk perceptions were used as mediating variables to examine the causal impact of teacher stress, and cognitive factors (job satisfaction, self-efficacy and emotional intensity) and their perceptions of COVID-19 on dependent variables (teaching methods and social relationships at school). The path analysis results showed that teacher stress was positively correlated with risk of contracting COVID-19 and higher stress scores indicated lower perception of EHM. Teacher's emotional intensity had an indirect effect on their perception of COVID-19 through the risk perceptions as mediator variable. The study also found that cognitive factors had an indirect effect on dependent variables through risk perception of contracting COVID-19 and EHM. The study highlights the importance of stress and presence of cognitive coping strategies (self-efficacy and emotional intensity) in school teachers [108]. The emotional competence and ability to handle conflicts of primary school teachers was examined in terms of socio-demographic (sex, age, have own children) and professional (teaching experience, type of school) variables and their ability to manage students (interpret student emotions, respect for students). Women scored higher than men in emotional competence and conflict handling capability. Age, children, years of teaching experience, and type of school had no differences in terms of emotional competence, classroom management and skill to deal with conflicts. The youngest teachers showed slightly higher sensitivity to develop learning environments that address student diversity. The results also indicated that teachers who loved their work were marginally more prepared to deal with conflicts [109].

Resilience has been identified as a major factor that has a negative effect on role conflict. In other words, high levels of resilience have a protective effect and reduces the occurrence of role conflict. Padmanabhanunni [110] conducted as study on teacher resilience and its relationship with role conflict, role ambiguity, life satisfaction, anxiety and depression. The results showed that resilience had a negative impact on anxiety, depression, and role conflict and ambiguity but a positive influence on life satisfaction. In another study conducted by Liu et al. [111], the association between job burnout, turnover intentions, and resilience was investigated in high school teachers. The results showed that resilience had a negative effect on job burnout and turnover intention, which again reiterates the idea that resilience is an effective coping strategy during conflict, and stress.

In addition to resilience, self-efficacy has been shown to manage conflicts, stress and turnover intentions in teachers and offers a protective effect against burnout during the pandemic [112, 113]. Teaching efficacy is directly related to teacher's self-efficacy which is the trust teachers have in their ability to help student learn, motivate, engage and attain high levels of academic achievement. Self-efficacy related to teaching (instructional strategies, classroom management and student engagement along with emotional regulation were examined as predictors for work-related burnout. The results showed that lower scores on self-efficacy related to instructional strategies led to higher burnout scores [112]. A study conducted by Lucker et al. [96] explored the sources of support that teachers felt were important to them. The teachers indicated in their survey responses that family, friends, pupil's student's parents, school management, coworkers were the most important individuals who supported them during the pandemic. The teachers also noted the different types of conflict and stress coping strategies, such as availability of reliable information, relaxation techniques (e.g., sports and yoga, activities in nature), experiencing appreciation and being with people who are valuable. The study showed that proactive coping was positively correlated with perceived self-efficacy. The results also showed that teachers who had higher levels of perceived self-efficacy and proactive coping were less likely to leave their jobs than those teachers who had higher levels of stress. Teaching efficacy on technological content knowledge (TCK) and overall satisfaction with personal lives were also shown to have beneficial effects on online teaching during the pandemic. The role of self-efficacy has also been examined with technological content knowledge, motivation (intrinsic and extrinsic) in the context of occupational stress (burnout and technostress/technological overload) and intentions to use online instruction. The results showed that teacher's self-efficacy intrinsic motivation negatively influenced their intention to continue the use of online instruction. Intrinsic motivation also had a negative impact on burnout and technostress. Burnout and technostress were significant mediators between intrinsic motivation and intention to continue the usage of online instruction.

Job satisfaction is the contentment and happiness an employee feels in the workplace with regards to their performance, productivity and overall well-being. Several studies have shown the positive effect of teacher's job satisfaction on various outcome variables, including conflict and stress management. A study conducted by Padmanabhanunni and Pretorius [97] used teaching satisfaction as a measure of job satisfaction. The results showed that teaching satisfaction had a negative relationship with role conflict, role ambiguity, depression, and negative aspect of psychological well-being and a positive association with life satisfaction. Both role conflict and role ambiguity had a positive association with anxiety and depression. Research has shown that employees who have high self-efficacy also have more job satisfaction. Hence, self-efficacy is an important predictor of job satisfaction as shown in the study by Bartosiewicz et al. [114]. The quantitative analyses showed that job satisfaction had a positive impact on work-related behaviors related to healthy type (committed, balanced, problem-solvers) where employees reported higher levels of self-efficacy scores when compared to burnout (high levels of pessimistic emotions and low mental resilience) and savings type (reduced level of motivation, limited levels of professional responsibility). In a study conducted by Punzalan [102], job satisfaction has also been shown to have a negative correlation with work family conflict and family work conflict.

10. Summary

This chapter presented the current research trends on the causes, consequences and management of conflicts occurring in PK-12 schools with teachers as the main focal point. The primary causes of conflict in schools is due to individual (e.g., self-efficacy, coping strategies), and contextual-level factors (e.g., organizational fairness, workplace climate, availability of interventions for stress management) [22, 26, 73, 95]. The majority of studies reviewed were either quantitative or qualitative research design. Future studies on conflicts in schools can focus on mixed-methods research designs to have richer data and deeper understanding of the factors under investigation. The research conducted in this topic can also investigate the role of workplace bullying as one of the antecedents for conflicts. Future research on conflicts can also utilize longitudinal research designs to study the role of individual and contextual-level factors on conflict management and resolution over a period of time. Furthermore, the research on conflicts with teachers as the focal point can benefit if interventions and strategies can be developed based on the source of conflict. The knowledge generated could be used by principals and school district administration to effectively manage and resolve conflicts in an appropriate and timely manner. The current body of empirical literature on conflicts in PK-12 schools is valuable. Further research on this topic would be beneficial to reduce the negative consequences of conflicts at micro and macro levels within school districts.

Author details

Parul Acharya
Department of Teacher Education, Leadership and Counseling, College of Education and Health Professions, Columbus State University, United States

*Address all correspondence to: acharya_parul@columbusstate.edu

References

[1] Litterer JA. Conflict in organization: A re-examination. The Academy of Management Journal. 1966;**9**(3):178-186. DOI: 10.2307/255117

[2] Pondy LR. A systems theory of organizational conflict. The Academy of Management Journal. 1966;**9**(3):246-256

[3] Fabunimi M, Alimba CN. Conflict in school climate: A synopsis of its nature, causes. Effects and management approaches. African Journal of Education Management. 2010;**13**(2):205-226

[4] Hoy WK, Tarter CJ. Organizational justice in schools: No justice without trust. The International Journal of Educational Management. 2004;**18**(4):250-259

[5] Gürcüoglu S, Uyar M. Examining the relationship between organizational conflict and organizational climate from the perspective of secondary education teachers. The Journal of Social Sciences Institute. 2020;**23**(43):229-254

[6] Akgöz EE, Cemaloğlu N. Views of administrators and teachers on conflict causes and resolution in secondary schools. The Journal of International Education Science. 2020;**22**(7):60-84

[7] Bauer J, Unterbrink T, Hack A, Pfeifer R, Buhl-Grießhaber V, Müller U, et al. Working conditions, adverse events and mental health problems in a sample of 949 German teachers. International Archives of Occupational Environmental Health. 2007;**80**:442-449

[8] Boström M, Björklund C, Bergström G, Nybergh L, Schäfer EL, Stigmar K, et al. Health and work environment among female and male Swedish elementary school teachers—A cross-sectional study. International Journal of Environment Research in Public Health. 2019;**17**(1):227. DOI: 10.3390/ijerph17010227. PMID: 31905608; PMCID: PMC6982179

[9] Kokkinos CM. Job stressors, personality and burnout in primary school teachers. British Journal of Educational Psychology. 2007;**77**:229-243

[10] Konukman F, Agbuğa B, Erdoğan S, Zorba E, Demirhan G, Yilmaz I. Teacher-coach role conflict in school-based physical education in USA: A literature review and suggestions for the future. Biomedical Human Kinetics. 2010;**2**:19-24

[11] Skaalvik EM, Skaalvik S. Teacher job satisfaction and motivation to leave the teaching profession: Relations with school context, feeling of belonging, and emotional exhaustion. Teaching and Teacher Education. 2011;**27**(6):1029-1038

[12] Vercambre MN, Brosselin P, Gilbert F, Nerrière E, Kovess-Masféty V. Individual and contextual covariates of burnout: A cross-sectional nationwide study of French teachers. BMC Public Health. 2009;**9**:333

[13] Baya A. The reasons of conflicts in school as an organization and finding some potential solutions in terms of school principals' perspective. Sakarya University Journal of Education. 2015;**5**(3):130-141

[14] Ghaffar A. Conflict in schools: Its causes & management strategies. Journal of Managerial Sciences. 2009;**3**(2):212-227

[15] Isa AA. Conflicts in organizations: Causes and consequences. Journal of Educational Policy and Entrepreneurial Research. 2015;**2**(11):54-59

[16] Jones TS. Conflict resolution education: The field, the findings, and the future. Conflict Resolution Quarterly. 2004;**22**(1-2):233-267

[17] Larasati R, Raharja S. Conflict management in improving school's effectiveness. In: Proceedings of the 3rd International Conference on Learning Innovation and Quality Education (ICLIQE 2019); Surakarta, Indonesia. 2019. pp. 191-197

[18] Mishra L. Peace education as a tool for effective conflict management in secondary schools in Odisha. Journal of Education. 2013;**3**(1):69-76

[19] Shanka EB, Thuo M. Conflict management and resolution strategies between teachers and school leaders in primary schools of Wolaita Zone, Ethiopia. Journal of Education and Practice. 2017;**8**(4):63-74

[20] Ertürk R. Conflict in schools: A qualitative study. Participatory Educational Research. 2022;**9**(1):251-270. Available from: https://dergipark.org.tr/en/download/article-file/1657226

[21] Schaufeli WB, Taris TW. A critical review of the job demands-resources model: Implications for improving work and health. In: Bauer GF, Hämmig O, editors. Bridging Occupational, Organizational and Public Health: A Transdisciplinary Approach. 1st ed. Berlin/Heidelberg, Germany: Springer Science + Business Media; 2014. pp. 43-68

[22] Maslach C. A multidimensional theory of burnout. Theories of organizational. Stress. 1998;**68**. Available from: https://www.researchgate.net/publication/280939428_A_Multidimensional_Theory_of_Burnout

[23] Schaufeli WB, Taris TW. The conceptualization and measurement of burnout: Common ground and worlds apart. Work and Stress. 2005;**19**(3):256-262

[24] Brunsting NC, Sreckovic MA, Lane KL. Special education teacher burnout: A synthesis of research from 1979 to 2013. Education and Treatment of Children. 2014;**37**(4):681-711. DOI: 10.1353/etc.2014.0032

[25] Iancu AE, Rusu A, Măroiu C, Păcurar R, Maricuțoiu LP. The effectiveness of interventions aimed at reducing teacher burnout: A meta-analysis. Educational Psychology Review. 2018;**30**(2):373-396. DOI: 10.1007/s10648-017-9420-8

[26] Park E-Y, Shin M. A meta-analysis of special education teachers' burnout. SAGE Open. 2020;**1**(2). DOI: 10.1177/2158244020918297

[27] Wisniewski L, Gargiulo RM. Occupational stress and burnout among special educators: A review of the literature. The Journal of Special Education. 1997;**31**(3):325-346. DOI: 10.1177/002246699703100303

[28] Brunsting NC, Bettini E, Rock ML, Royer DJ, Common EA, Lane KL, et al. Burnout of special educators serving students with emotional-behavioral disorders: A longitudinal study. Remedial and Special Education. 2022;**43**(3):160-171. DOI: 10.1177/07419325211030562

[29] Nwoko J, Emeto T, Malau-Aduli AEO. A systematic review of the factors that influence teachers' occupational wellbeing. International Journal of Environmental Research and Public Health. June 2023;**20**(12):6070. DOI: 10.3390/ijerph20126070

[30] Mijakoski D, Cheptea D, Marca SC, Shoman Y, Caglayan C, Bugge MD, et al. Determinants of burnout among

teachers: A systematic review of longitudinal studies. International Journal of Environmental Research in Public Health. 2022;**19**(9):5776. DOI: 10.3390/ijerph19095776

[31] Colquitt JA. On the dimensionality of organizational justice: A construct validation of a measure. Journal of Applied Psychology. 2001;**86**(3):386-400. DOI: 10.1037/0021-9010.86.3.386

[32] Adeyemi TO. Principals management of conflicts in public secondary schools in Ondo State, Nigeria: A critical survey. Educational Research and Review. 2009;**4**(9):418-426

[33] Özgan H. The relationships between organizational justice, confidence, commitment, and evaluating the manager and the perceptions of conflict management at the context of organizational behavior. Educational Sciences: Theory & Practice. 2011;**11**(1):241-247

[34] Sehgal M, Verma J. A study of perception of organizational justice in relation to organizational commitment and occupational stress in female school teachers. Journal of Psychosocial Research. 2017;**12**(2):521-529

[35] Loerbroks A, Meng H, Chen ML, Herr R, Angerer P, Li J. Primary school teachers in China: Associations of organizational justice and effort-reward imbalance with burnout and intentions to leave the profession in a cross-sectional sample. International Archives Occupational and Environment Health. 2014;**87**(7):695-703. DOI: 10.1007/s00420-013-0912-7

[36] Capone V, Petrillo G. Teachers' perceptions of fairness, well-being and burnout. International Journal of Educational Management. 2016;**6**:864-880

[37] Li Y. Building affective commitment to organization among Chinese university teachers: The roles of organizational justice and job burnout. Educational Assessment, Evaluation and Accountability. 2014;**26**(2):135-152

[38] Andela M, Truchot D. The impact of distributive and procedural justice on burnout: Does it affect French and German teachers differently? International Journal of Culture and Mental Health. 2017;**10**(3):276-284. DOI: 10.1080/17542863.2017.1300592

[39] Kamran M, Thomas M. The effect of teachers' perception of organizational justice on their job stress. International journal of organizational. Leadership. 2021;**10**(Special Issue):89-98

[40] Cohen J, McCabe L, Michelli NM, Pickeral T. School climate: Research, policy, practice, and teacher education. Teachers College Record: The Voice of Scholarship in Education. 2009;**111**(1):180-213. DOI: 10.1177/016146810911100108

[41] Ingersoll R, Strong M. The impact of induction and mentoring programs for beginning teachers: A critical review of the research. Review of Educational Research. 2011;**81**(2):201-233

[42] Oresajo NO. Conflict management in school organization in Nigeria. International Journal of Development and Management Review. 2015;**10**(1):166-175. Available from: https://www.ajol.info/index.php/ijdmr/article/view/120975

[43] Otrębski W. The correlation between organizational (school) climate and teacher job satisfaction-the type of educational institution moderating role. International Journal of Environmental Research in Public Health. 2022;**19**(11):6520. DOI: 10.3390/ijerph19116520

[44] Gray C, Wilcox G, Nordstokke D. Teacher mental health, school climate, inclusive education and student learning: A review. Canadian Psychology/Psychologie canadienne. 2017;**58**(3):203-210. DOI: 10.1037/cap0000117

[45] Sönmez S, Kolaşınlı IB. The effect of preschool teachers' stress states on classroom climate. Education. 2021;**49**(2):3-13,190-202. DOI: 10.1080/03004279.2019.1709528

[46] Lambert RG, McCarthy CJ, Fitchett PG, Eyal M. Examining elementary teachers' risk for occupational stress: Associations with teacher, school, and state policy variables. Teachers College Record. 2018;**120**(12):1-42. DOI: 10.1177/016146811812001205

[47] Nalipay MJN. What aspects of school climate matter most to Asian teachers' job satisfaction and well-being? Evidence from the TALIS 2018. Teachers College Record. 2023;**125**(3):264-288. DOI: 10.1177/01614681231171804

[48] Nguyen LT, Dang VT, Pham HT. The effects of school climate on high school teacher stress and self-efficacy in Ho Chi Minh City. Educational Psychology. 2023;**43**(1):57-77. DOI: 10.1080/01443410.2022.2128054

[49] Hu BY, Li Y, Wang C, Reynolds BL. The relation between school climate and preschool teacher stress: The mediating role of teachers' self-efficacy. Journal of Educational Administration. 2019;**57**(6):748-767

[50] Ebert DD, Lehr D, Bo L, Riper H, Cuijpers P, Andersson G, et al. Efficacy of an internet-based problem-solving training for teachers: Results of a randomized controlled trial. Scandinavian Journal of Work, Environment & Health. 2014;**40**(6):582-596. DOI: 10.5271/sjweh.3449

[51] Maricuțoiu LP, Sava FA, Butta O. The effectiveness of controlled interventions on employees' burnout: A meta-analysis. Journal of Occupational and Organizational Psychology. 2016;**89**(1):1-27. DOI: 10.1111/joop.12099

[52] Jeon L, Ardeleanu K. Work climate in early care and education and teachers' stress: Indirect associations through emotion regulation. Early Education and Development. 2020;**31**(7):1031-1051. DOI: 10.1080/10409289.2020.1776809

[53] Beltman S, Mansfield C, Price A. Thriving not just surviving: A review of research on teacher resilience. Educational Research Review. 2011;**6**:185-207. DOI: 10.1016/j.edurev.2011.09.001

[54] Demirdağ S. The relationship between primary school administrators' ethical leadership and conflict management strategies: The perceptions of substitute teachers. Turkish Studies-International Periodical for the Languages, Literature and History of Turkish or Turkic. 2016;**11**(3):879-894. DOI: 10.7827/TurkishStudies.9250

[55] Demirkaya Y. Teacher perceptions of school principals' conflict management strategies and communication styles (master's thesis). Burdur: Mehmet Akif Ersoy University Institute of Educational Sciences; 2012

[56] Msila V. Conflict management and school leadership. Journal of Communication. 2012;**3**(1):25-34

[57] Okotoni O, Okotoni A. Conflict management in secondary schools in Osun State, Nigeria. Nordic Journal of African Studies. 2003;**12**(1):23-38

[58] Pas ET, Bradshaw CP, Hershfeldt PA. Teacher and school-level predictors of teacher efficacy and burnout: Identifying potential areas for support. Journal of

School Psychology. 2012;**50**(1):129-145. DOI: 10.1016/j.jsp.2011.07.003

[59] Uzun T, Ayık A. Relationship between communication competence and conflict management styles of school principals. Eurasian Journal of Educational Research. 2017;**68**:167-186

[60] Berkovich I, Eyal O. Help me if you can: Psychological distance and help-seeking intentions in employee–supervisor relations. Stress and Health: Journal of the International Society for the Investigation of Stress. 2018;**34**(3):425-434. DOI: 10.1002/smi.2802

[61] Herman KC, Sebastian J, Reinke WM, Huang FL. Individual and school predictors of teacher stress, coping, and wellness during the COVID-19 pandemic. School Psychology. 2021;**36**(6):483-493. DOI: 10.1037/spq0000456

[62] Ma K, Liang L, Chutiyami M, Nicoll S, Khaerudin T, Van Ha X. COVID-19 pandemic-related anxiety, stress, and depression among teachers: A systematic review and meta-analysis. Work. 2022;**73**(1):3-27. DOI: 10.3233/WOR-220062

[63] Maas J, Schoch S, Scholz U, Rackow P, Schüler J, Wegner M, et al. School principals' social support and teachers' basic need satisfaction: The mediating role of job demands and job resources. Social Psychology of Education. 2022;**25**(6):1545-1562. DOI: 10.1007/s11218-022-09730-6

[64] Uchendu CC, Anijaobi-Idem FN, Odigwe FN. Conflict management and organizational performance in secondary schools in cross river state, Nigeria. Research Journal in Organizational Psychology and Educational Studies. 2013;**2**(2):67-71

[65] Rave R, Itzchakov G, Weinstein N, et al. How to get through hard times: Principals' listening buffers teachers' stress on turnover intention and promotes organizational citizenship behavior. Current Psychology. 2023;**42**:24233-24248. DOI: 10.1007/s12144-022-03529-6

[66] Gooden C, Zelkowski J, Smith FA. A systematic literature review on factors of stress, burnout and job satisfaction of secondary grades teachers at time of professional crisis. The Clearing House: A Journal of Educational Strategies, Issues and Ideas. 2023;**96**(5):162-171

[67] Willis L, Reynolds KJ, Lee E. Being well at work: The impact of organizational climate and social identity on employee stress and self-esteem over time. European Journal of Work and Organizational Psychology. 2019;**28**(3):399-413. DOI: 10.1080/1359432X.2019.1587409

[68] van derWal MM, Oolbekkink-Marchand HW, Schaap H, Meijer PC. Impact of early career teachers' professional identity tensions. Teaching and Teacher Education. 2019;**80**:59-70

[69] Slay HS, Smith DA. Professional identity construction: Using narrative to understand the negotiation of professional and stigmatized cultural identities. Human Relations. 2011;**64**(1):85-107

[70] Day C, Stobart G, Sammons P, Kington A. Variations in the work and lives of teachers: Relative and relational effectiveness. Teachers and Teaching. 2006;**12**(2):169-192

[71] Padmanabhanunni A, Pretorius TB. Job satisfaction goes a long way: The mediating role of teaching satisfaction in the relationship between role stress and indices of psychological well-being in the time of COVID-19. International Journal of Environmental Research in Public Health. 2022;**19**(24):17071. DOI: 10.3390/ijerph192417071

[72] Wolgast A, Fischer N. You are not alone: Colleague support and goal-oriented cooperation as resources to reduce teachers' stress. Social Psychology of Education. 2017;**20**:97-114. DOI: 10.1007/s11218-017-9366-1

[73] Baptista MN, Cardoso HF. Do organizational support and occupational stressors influence burnout in teachers? Baptista & Cardoso Avaliação Psicológica. 2021;**20**(4). DOI: 10.15689/ap.2021.2004.21998.05

[74] Boyle LH, Mosley KC, McCarthy CJ. New teachers' risk for stress: Associations with mentoring supports. International Journal of Mentoring and Coaching in Education. 2022;**12**(1):95-110

[75] Kapadia K, Coca V, Easton JQ. Keeping New Teachers: A First Look at Influences of Induction in the Chicago Public Schools. Consortium on Chicago School Research. Chicago: University of Chicago; 2007. Available from: https://core.ac.uk/download/pdf/71348059.pdf

[76] Ronfeldt M, McQueen K. Does new teacher induction really improve retention? Journal of Teacher Education. 2017;**68**(4):394-410

[77] Antoniou A, Efthymiou V, Polychroni F, Kofa O. Occupational stress in mainstream and special needs primary school teachers and its relationship with self-efficacy. Educational Studies. 2023;**49**(1):200-217. DOI: 10.1080/03055698.2020.1837080

[78] Reilly E, Dhingra K, Boduszek D. Teachers' self-efficacy beliefs, self-esteem, and job stress as determinants of job satisfaction. International Journal of Educational Management. 2013;**28**(4):365-378

[79] Schwarzer R, Hallum S. Perceived teacher self-efficacy as a predictor of job stress and burnout. Applied Psychology: An International Review. 2008;**57**(Suppl 1):152-171. DOI: 10.1111/j.1464-0597.2008.00359.x

[80] Zhang L. The relationship between self-efficacy and job burnout of ideological and political teacher based on quantitative and qualitative analysis. NeuroQuantology. 2018;**16**(6). DOI: 10.14704/nq.2018.16.6.1580

[81] Betoret DF, Artiga GA. Barriers perceived by teachers at work, coping strategies, self-efficacy and burnout. Spanish Journal of Psychology. 2010;**13**(2):637-654. DOI: 10.1017/s1138741600002316

[82] Yu X, Wang P, Zhai X, Dai H, Yang Q. The effect of work stress on job burnout among teachers: The mediating role of self-efficacy. Social Indicators Research. 2015;**122**(3):701-708. DOI: 10.1007/s11205-014-0716-5

[83] Putwain DW, von der Embse NP. Teacher self-efficacy moderates the relations between imposed pressure from imposed curriculum changes and teacher stress. Educational Psychology. 2019;**39**(1):51-64. DOI: 10.1080/01443410.2018.1500681

[84] Jentsch A, Hoferichter F, Blömeke S, König J, Kaiser G. Investigating teachers' job satisfaction, stress and working environment: The roles of self-efficacy and school leadership. Psychology in the Schools. 2022;**60**(3):679-690

[85] Jeon L, Buettner CK, Grant AA. Early childhood teachers' psychological well-being: Exploring potential predictors of depression, stress, and emotional exhaustion. Early Education and Development. 2018;**29**(1):53-69. DOI: 10.1080/10409289.2017.1341806

[86] Li S. The effect of teacher self-efficacy, teacher resilience, and

emotion regulation on teacher burnout: A mediation model. Frontiers of. Psychology. 2023;**24**(14):1185079. DOI: 10.3389/fpsyg.2023.1185079

[87] Klassen R, Wilson E, Siu AFY, Hannok W, Wong MW, Wongsri N, et al. Preservice teachers' work stress, self-efficacy, and occupational commitment in four countries. European Journal of Psychology of Education. 2013;**28**(4):1289-1309. Available from: http://www.jstor.org/stable/23580909

[88] Helms-Lorenz M, Maulana R. Influencing the psychological well-being of beginning teachers across three years of teaching: Self-efficacy, stress causes, job tension and job discontent. Educational Psychology. 2016;**36**(3):569-594

[89] Roberts AM, LoCasale-Crouch J, Hamre BK, Jamil FM. Preschool teachers' self-efficacy, burnout, and stress in online professional development: A mixed methods approach to understand change. Journal of Early Childhood Teacher Education. 2020;**41**(3):262-283. DOI: 10.1080/10901027.2019.1638851

[90] Aguayo F, Olga S, Rodríguez M, Luisa M, Miguel MM, Pino-Juste M. Effective mindfulness-based stress reduction in teachers: A bibliometric analysis. The International Journal of Pedagogy and Curriculum. 2017;**24**(1):49-62. DOI: 10.18848/2327-7963/CGP/v24i01/49-62

[91] von der Embse N, Ryan SV, Gibbs T, Mankin A. Teacher stress interventions: A systematic review. Psychology in the Schools. 2019;**56**(8):1328-1343. DOI: 10.1002/pits.22279

[92] Good DJ, Lyddy CJ, Glomb TM, Bono JE, Brown KW, Duffy MK, et al. Contemplating mindfulness at work: An integrative review. Journal of Management. 2016;**42**(1):114-142. DOI: 10.1177/0149206315617003

[93] Baer RA, Smith GT, Lykins E, Button D, Krietemeyer J, Sauer S, et al. Construct validity of the five-facet mindfulness questionnaire in meditating and nonmeditating samples. Assessment. 2008;**15**(3):329-342. DOI: 10.1177/1073191107313003

[94] Aundrea HT, Bostain NS. The effect of mindfulness techniques on teacher resilience as moderated by conscientiousness. Journal of Educational Research and Practice. 2021;**11**(1):81-94

[95] Molina CE, Lemberger-Truelove ME, Zieher AK. School Counselor consultation effects on teachers' mindfulness, stress, and relationships. Professional School Counseling. 2022;**26**(1a). DOI: 10.1177/2156759X221086749

[96] Lücker P, Kästner A, Hannich A, Schmeyers L, Lücker J, Hoffmann W. Stress, coping and considerations of leaving the profession-a cross-sectional online survey of teachers and school principals after two years of the pandemic. International Journal of Environmental Research in Public Health. 2022;**19**(23):16122. DOI: 10.3390/ijerph192316122

[97] Pretorius TB, Padmanabhanunni A, Isaacs SA, Jackson K. Perceived vulnerability to disease and the relationship with teacher satisfaction in South Africa during COVID-19: The serial role of burnout, role conflict, and ambiguity. Behavioral Sciences. 2022;**12**(6):160. DOI: 10.3390/bs12060160

[98] Yazdi MT, Motallebzadeh K, Ashraf H. The role of teacher's

self-efficacy as a predictor of Iranian EFL teacher's burnout. Journal of Language Teaching and Research. 2014;**5**(5):1198-1204

[99] Gómez-Domínguez V, Gómez-Domínguez T, Navarro-Mateu D, Giménez-Espert MC. The influence of COVID-19 and psychosocial risks on burnout and psychosomatic health problems in non-university teachers in Spain during the peak of the pandemic regressions vs. fsQCA. Sustainability. 2022;**14**(20):13030. DOI: 10.3390/su142013030

[100] Boneh MZ, Feniger-Schaal R, Bivas TA, Danial-Saad A. Teachers under stress during the COVID-19: Cultural differences. Teachers and Teaching. 2022;**28**(2):164-187. DOI: 10.1080/13540602.2021.2017275

[101] Santiago ISD, Dos-Santos EP, da Silva JA, Cavalcante Y, Júnior GJ, de Souza Costa AR, et al. The impact of the COVID-19 pandemic on the mental health of teachers and its possible risk factors: A systematic review. International Journal of Environmental Research and Public Health. 2023;**20**(3):1747. DOI: 10.3390/ijerph20031747

[102] Punzalan JM et al. Social support, work-family conflict and job satisfaction of teachers during COVID-19 pandemic. North American Journal of Psychology. 2023;**25**(1)

[103] Padmanabhanunni A, Pretorius TB. Teacher burnout in the time of COVID-19: Antecedents and psychological consequences. International Journal of Environmental Research in Public Health. 2023;**20**(5):4204. DOI: 10.3390/ijerph20054204

[104] Baker CNH, Peele M, Daniels M, Saybe K, Whalen S. The experience of COVID-19 and its impact on teachers' mental health coping, and teaching. School Psychology Review. 2021;**50**(4):491-504. DOI: 10.1080/2372966X.2020.1855473

[105] Chang ML, Gaines RE, Mosley KC. Effects of autonomy support and emotion regulation on teacher burnout in the era of the COVID-19 pandemic. Frontiers in Psychology. 2022;**25**(13):846290. DOI: 10.3389/fpsyg.2022.846290

[106] Truzoli R, Pirola V, Conte S. The impact of risk and protective factors on online teaching experience in high school Italian teachers during the COVID-19 pandemic. Journal of Computing and Assistive Learning. 2021;**37**(4):940-952. DOI: 10.1111/jcal.12533

[107] Hidalgo-Andrade P, Hermosa-Bosano C, Paz C. Teachers' mental health and self-reported coping strategies during the COVID-19 pandemic in Ecuador: A mixed-methods study. Psychology Research and Behavior Management. 2021;**14**:933-944. DOI: 10.2147/PRBM.S314844

[108] Porru A, Dicataldo R, Leo I, Roch M, Lucangeli D. Back to school: Italian teachers' perceptions of the impact of COVID-19 on personal and social well-being and teaching methods. International Journal of Environmental Research and Public Health. 2022;**19**(18):11652. DOI: 10.3390/ijerph191811652

[109] Ponce RS, Luján EL, Sarimento AYS, Beut J, G. Emotional competences of primary education teachers: A need in school post COVID-19. European Journal of Investigation in Health Psychology and Education. 2023;**13**(10):1961-1985

[110] Padmanabhanunni A, Pretorius TB, Khamisa N. The role of resilience in the

relationship between role stress and psychological well-being during the COVID-19 pandemic: A cross-sectional study. BMC Psychology. 2023;**11**(1):45. DOI: 10.1186/s40359-023-01082-w

[111] Liu F, Chen H, Xu J, Wen Y, Fang T. Exploring the relationships between resilience and turnover intention in Chinese high school teachers: Considering the moderating role of job burnout. International Journal of Environmental Research and Public Health. 2021;**18**(12):6418. DOI: 10.3390/ijerph18126418

[112] Daniel E, Bergen PV. Teacher burnout during COVID-19: Associations with instructional self-efficacy but not emotion regulation. Teachers and Teaching. 2023;**29**(3):310-328. DOI: 10.1080/13540602.2023.2179615

[113] Kareem J, Valaramathi BS, Tantia V. Influence of teacher occupational stress on self-efficacy: Evidences from the pre- and during-COVID-19 periods. International Journal of Virtual and Personal Learning Environments. 2022;**22**(1):1-17

[114] Bartosiewicz A, Łuszczki E, Zaręba L, Kuchciak M, Bobula G, Dereń K, et al. Assessment of job satisfaction, self-efficacy, and the level of professional burnout of primary and secondary school teachers in Poland during the COVID-19 pandemic. Peer Journal. 2022;**10**:e13349. DOI: 10.7717/peerj.13349

Chapter 6

Harmony amidst Turmoil: Navigating Conflict with Mindfulness

Zohreh Hosseinzadeh

Abstract

Conflict can lead to lower employee productivity and job satisfaction. By incorporating mindfulness practices into the workplace, organizations create an environment where employees can respond thoughtfully and promote a harmonious and cooperative atmosphere. Mindfulness is the act of paying attention in a particular way: on purpose, in the present moment, and non-judgmentally. It enables us to observe our thoughts, emotions, and sensations without being carried away by them. The benefits of mindfulness in the workplace are enormous. It decreases stress levels and turnover rates, improves productivity, and fosters innovation. Mindfulness improves negotiation, problem-solving, and decision-making. It also promotes a culture of respect, compassion, and empathy. It allows individuals to recognize and regulates harmful behaviors. Mindful leadership enhances feedback loops and communication channels. Studies show a positive correlation between leader mindfulness and employee well-being and performance. Clear roles, expectations, and conflict resolution skills that promote collaboration and discourage competition are some of its benefits. Some companies, such as Google, have successfully implemented mindfulness programs to reduce conflict and improve employee well-being, performance, and creativity. Mindfulness allows for better empathy, understanding, and open communication during conflicts. Open communication and active listening foster trust and prevent misunderstandings during conflict situations.

Keywords: mindfulness, negotiation, problem-solving, decision-making, leader mindfulness, conflict organization management

1. Introduction

Conflict can make employees less productive and satisfied with their jobs, resulting in lower performance. Unresolved conflict tends to fester and grow, making it even more challenging to resolve in the future. Taking a positive approach toward conflicts is advantageous and results in a greater sense of connectivity with colleagues at the workplace.

The promotion of prosocial attitudes and behaviors, as well as the attenuation of antisocial behaviors linked with conflict, has been demonstrated through the implementation of mindfulness. Mindfulness facilitates constructive conflict management, fostering collaboration, and avoiding avoidance [1]. The practice of mindfulness has been found to positively impact an individual's ability to regulate their emotions, resulting in a decrease in emotional exhaustion and an increase in overall job satisfaction [2]. Individuals with a high level of mindfulness tend to utilize a broader range of contextual details and employ their metacognitive abilities to reassess conflicts to demonstrate consideration for others [1].

2. What is mindfulness?

Mindfulness rooted in Buddhist meditation has entered the psychology mainstream, partly through the work of Jon Kabat-Zinn and his Mindfulness-Based Stress Reduction (MBSR) program. Jon Kabat-Zinn says mindfulness is "paying attention in a particular way: on purpose, in the present moment, and non-judgmentally" [3].

By cultivating mindfulness, we can develop a greater sense of clarity, calmness, and connection to ourselves and the world around us. It allows us to observe our thoughts, emotions, and sensations without getting carried away by them. Instead of reacting automatically, we can respond to situations more intentionally and wisely. Mindfulness is a quality that every human being already possesses. It is not something individuals must conjure up; they just have to learn how to access it.

Introducing mindfulness into the workplace is a beneficial undertaking on multiple fronts. It is a moral obligation to prioritize the health and adaptability of all staff members. Moreover, mindfulness is a wise commercial venture that yields fruitful returns. It can facilitate a decrease in stress levels, a reduction in turnover rates, an improvement in productivity, an attraction of top-tier talent, and an increase in innovation.

2.1 Individual mindfulness and organizational mindfulness

The construct of individual mindfulness encompasses a variety of components, namely observing, describing, acting with awareness, accepting without judgment, and non-reacting to inner experiences. Organizational mindfulness is defined by a group of five essential precepts: an unrelenting fixation on failures, a disinclination to oversimplify, an increased awareness of operations, an unwavering dedication to resilience, and a profound respect for expertise. It helps organizations detect early signs of approaching threats and enables more rapid responses. Mindfulness can aid organizations in identifying and resolving issues before they become major concerns, while also fostering innovation by encouraging exploration of new solutions and perspectives [4]. By providing cues regarding the organization's expectations, incentives, and assistance, organizational mindfulness constructs a framework that helps individuals understand the context within the organization.

2.1.1 The effects of individual mindfulness

Individual mindfulness helps members of organizations obtain an objective perspective even in stressful situations. This ability can facilitate effective communication among individuals in such situations and promote a willingness to respect and defer to expertise. Individual mindfulness makes individuals more sensitive to other members' perspectives.

The cultivation of individual mindfulness is a significant factor in the facilitation of inventive approaches to problem-solving and acquisition of knowledge, subsequently developing novel insights that may be effectively disseminated throughout the organization. Organizational mindfulness implies individual mindfulness but not vice versa [5].

2.2 Mindfulness in modern workplaces. Where fast-paced environments often lead to reactive behaviors

In today's fast-paced and ever-changing work settings, the value of mindfulness is becoming more and more evident. The rapid pace of technological advancements, coupled with the constant stream of information and tasks, has created an atmosphere where encourages giving priority to responsive actions. In such a dynamic setting, the practice of mindfulness offers a valuable antidote to the impulsivity and stress that can undermine effective conflict resolution and overall well-being.

In the hustle and bustle of modern workplaces, employees frequently find themselves caught in a cycle of reacting to stimuli without thoughtful consideration. Emails must be answered promptly, meetings attended, deadlines met, high expectations, and a never-ending to-do list can result in chronic stress, which not only takes a toll on our mental and physical well-being but also affects our ability to handle conflicts effectively. When stress levels are high, our ability to regulate emotions and think rationally can become compromised.

This culture of immediacy can lead to knee-jerk reactions and impulsive responses, particularly in situations involving conflicts. People might respond to conflicts hastily, driven by emotions or external pressures, rather than taking the time to analyze the situation from a holistic perspective.

Mindfulness encourages individuals to pause, reflect, and respond intentionally rather than reactively. By cultivating mindfulness, employees can develop a heightened awareness of their thoughts, emotions, and physical sensations. This awareness provides the mental space necessary to assess situations more objectively, leading to more thoughtful and strategic conflict resolution.

Furthermore, mindfulness equips individuals with the ability to manage stress more effectively. Modern workplaces are notorious for their high-stress environments, which can exacerbate conflicts and impede their resolution. Mindfulness practices, such as deep breathing and meditation, help individuals regulate their stress responses and prevent emotional overwhelm. As a result, conflicts can be approached with a calmer and clearer mindset, enhancing the likelihood of finding constructive solutions.

The impact of mindfulness is not limited to individuals; it extends to the overall workplace culture. When both leaders and employees adopt mindfulness practices, it fosters an environment where open communication, empathy, and collaboration thrive. This culture of mindfulness promotes active listening and discourages knee-jerk reactions, creating a space where conflicts can be addressed with mutual respect and understanding.

In a world dominated by speed and constant demands, the practice of mindfulness offers a path toward effective conflict resolution, improved decision-making, successful negotiation, and enhanced overall well-being. By incorporating mindfulness practices into a workplace's framework, organizations can empower their employees to respond thoughtfully, manage stress, and promote a friendly and cooperative work environment.

3. Negotiation effectiveness

Negotiations are a critical means of conflict resolution in both organizational and personal settings. Negotiation effectiveness is associated with age, mindfulness, emotional intelligence, extraversion, openness, conscientiousness, achievement motivation, integrating, dominating, and compromising negotiation styles.

Negotiation styles have been linked to negotiation effectiveness. The most effective negotiation style combines compromising, integrating, and dominating styles [6]. Negotiators who possess a high level of emotional intelligence (EI) are capable of acquiring a broader and more comprehensive array of information regarding their opponent's essential interests, accurately gauging risks, employing strategies that involve managing their own emotions or the emotions of their counterparts, and evoking desirable emotions in those counterparts.

Effective negotiation requires that all parties involved possess a comprehensive comprehension of the interests and preferences of their respective counterparts, in addition to a meticulous recognition of their emotional states. The capacity to understand subtle communication cues may be useful for negotiators and could assist in guiding or avoiding potential obstacles [6]. The practice of meditation has been linked to superior abilities in compromising, obliging, and integration, particularly in situations where the interests of the other party are of significant importance. Conversely, meditators have been seen to exhibit reduced inclination toward the utilization of the avoiding and dominating styles, which tend to give more importance to one's own interests over that of the other party.

Openness and awareness, which are mindfulness's most essential components, positively affect negotiation effectiveness. Individuals with greater openness tend to display greater flexibility and divergent thinking and this could help broaden negotiations to develop better offers for themselves and others. And, negotiators who are more aware tend to outperform their less aware peers, achieving more tasks and making more preparations for complex tasks.

3.1 Mindfulness can lead to more successful negotiations

Practicing mindfulness may improve the negotiator and mediator's capacity to listen closely to themselves and others. Reb et al.'s [7] study examined how mindfulness influenced the results obtained in distributive negotiations. Meditating people are more effective in negotiation and associated variables such as EI. Meditators have greater negotiating effectiveness than non-meditators with similar sociodemographic characteristics [6]. The greater capacity for observation and awareness of the physical stimuli, thoughts, feelings, and bodily sensations involved in a negotiation process can lead to a constructive climate of joviality and greater openness and flexibility in the search for solutions.

Incorporating facets of mindfulness, such as purpose, presence, acceptance, and connectedness, may improve the effectiveness of the negotiator and may make the experience more satisfactory and stimulating for the negotiator. The greater capacity of observation and the awareness of the physical stimuli, thoughts, feelings, and bodily sensations involved in a negotiation process can lead to an attitude of "firm flexibility" when negotiating. For example, meditators act with awareness and without reacting with "automatic pilot" (The ability to act without really thinking happens when behavior becomes over-learned).

Mindfulness training affords negotiators the ability to sustain their attention over prolonged periods, process a more significant number of signals emanating from their counterparts, and maintain superior emotional regulation. Additionally, meditation can heighten one's sense of empathy, thereby contributing to a deeper comprehension of the counterpart's perspective and fostering the development of trust.

Improved cognitive abilities and enhanced interpersonal behavior resulting from mindfulness training can contribute to achieving more effective negotiation outcomes.

4. Problem solving and mindfulness

Solving problems involves cognitive and behavioral domains encompassing advanced cognitive skills, such as ascertaining, selecting, and formulating efficacious resolutions [8]. Ren et al. [9] found that individuals who participated in meditation practice demonstrated an increased ability to solve previously unresolved problems compared to those in the control condition.

Mindfulness has been shown to have a positive effect on problem-solving skills. When individuals practice mindfulness, they cultivate a state of non-judgmental awareness and attention to the present moment. This phenomenon facilitates the reduction of cognitive and emotional disruptions, thus enhancing the ability of individuals to concentrate more effectively on their current tasks.

Research studies have demonstrated that individuals who regularly practice mindfulness are better able to approach problem-solving tasks with clarity and creativity. They exhibit improved cognitive flexibility, which enables them to consider multiple perspectives and alternative solutions. Mindfulness also helps to enhance working memory, allowing individuals to hold and manipulate information more effectively, ultimately leading to better problem-solving outcomes. Furthermore, mindfulness has been found to reduce stress and improve emotional regulation. This is particularly beneficial in problem-solving situations, as stress and negative emotions can hinder the ability to think clearly and creatively. By promoting a calm and focused mindset, mindfulness allows individuals to approach problems with a greater sense of composure and resilience [10].

The literature suggests that mindfulness has the potential to enhance problem-solving abilities, particularly in resolving insight problems [9, 11]. Additionally, mindfulness has been found to aid in identifying innovative solutions to given problems [12]. These findings imply that mindfulness may influence creativity, in terms of both convergent and divergent thinking processes. As evidenced by the research conducted by Ostafin and Kassman [11], consisting of a sample size of 157 individuals, trait mindfulness was found to be a significant predictor of enhanced insight problem-solving capabilities. Furthermore, mindfulness training was observed to exert a positive influence on this ability. Similarly, Gesell et al. [13] reported that their own investigations suggest that mindfulness is linked to favorable outcomes in the context of interpersonal relationships, as evidenced by heightened problem-solving skills, a decreased tendency toward withdrawal, and an increased sense of intimacy.

According to Dr. Natalia Karelaia, Assistant Professor of Decision Sciences at the INSEAD Business School in Paris, mindfulness is incorporated into every business area where strong decisions are required [14].

There are four main stages to making an effective decision, and mindfulness helps with all of them:

1. The process of making a decision can sometimes benefit from refraining from action and instead observing the course of events. Mindfulness can provide valuable insight, courage, and patience to pursue this course of action when it is deemed most appropriate. When a decision is necessary, mindfulness can aid in delineating objectives, generating alternative options, and avoiding the irrational escalation of a previously misguided decision. A practical method for avoiding sunk-cost bias is applying mindfulness. The irrational inclination to persist with a particular course of action solely due to prior investment of time, effort, or finances is a common phenomenon. An instance of this tendency is the reluctance to divest shares of a floundering company in anticipation of a future price rebound, which amounts to a fruitless attempt to recover sunk costs. Additionally, the practice of mindfulness can be instrumental in enabling individuals to make reasonable decisions that align with their overarching objectives and fundamental ethical principles.

2. Mindfulness techniques can be utilized effectively to mitigate the issue of information overload by enhancing working memory and cognition. Furthermore, practicing mindfulness can facilitate the concentration of one's efforts toward acquiring the most pertinent data available, which is more likely to adhere to a sound decision-making framework and align with one's long-term aspirations. Avoiding habitual search patterns engendered by mindfulness can augment the prospect of uncovering original or unforeseen concepts. Additionally, the contextualization of information can be facilitated through the enhancement of one's overall perspective *via* mindfulness techniques. As articulated by Dr. Karelaia, mindful decision-makers are more prone to acknowledging the limitations of their knowledge and objectively evaluating uncertainty. Indeed, empirical research has indicated that individuals who exhibit greater mindfulness possess a heightened tolerance for ambiguity and a greater propensity for decisive action when confronted with difficult choices amidst many unknown variables.

3. Mindfulness has been shown to reduce cognitive rigidity, which refers to the inclination to make decisions based on habitual thought patterns. Such cognitive rigidity can significantly impede decision-making and constrain one's thinking. Mindfulness also facilitates the ability to make more rational decisions by mitigating emotional biases. This is achieved by fostering awareness of one's emotional landscape and enabling one to recognize when it is starting to influence their decision-making. Mindful individuals also tend to possess heightened intuition, which stems from unconscious mental processes and can be instrumental in managing complexity and ambiguity. It often gives rise to innovative "Eureka or Aha!" moments. Mindfulness notably promotes the resilience and courage necessary to execute decisions effectively.

4. The final stage of the decision-making process could reasonably be considered the most crucial, namely, incorporating lessons learned from experience. Acknowledging mistakes can be a challenging task. However, mindfulness can somewhat facilitate this procedure, owing to its ability to diminish defensiveness and foster courage and resilience.

DOI: http://dx.doi.org/10.5772/intechopen.1003050

The phenomenon of mindfulness has been established as a significant concept in the field of psychology, as it guarantees individuals possess a greater propensity for acquiring appropriate insights from their experiences. It is a widely accepted norm that individuals attribute their previous accomplishments to their own proficiency while ascribing their past disappointments to external factors beyond their control. The occurrence of overconfidence can result in extremely unfavorable outcomes in both organizational and entrepreneurial settings. Individuals who exhibit mindfulness are more inclined to detach themselves from their ego, thereby fostering an environment that is more receptive to negative feedback. Hence, decision-makers who practice mindfulness are able to acquire knowledge in an impartial manner.

5. Culture of respect and compassion

Mindfulness in organizational and group conflict resolution is highly beneficial as it promotes a culture of respect and compassion. When individuals cultivate mindfulness in their interactions with others, they are able to approach conflicts with a sense of empathy and understanding. This mindset helps to foster a more conducive environment for resolving disagreements and building positive relationships.

By practicing mindfulness, individuals are encouraged to pay attention to their thoughts emotions, and conflict situations. This heightened self-awareness allows them to recognize and regulate any negative or harmful behaviors that may arise. Instead of reacting impulsively, it encourages individuals to recognize and manage their biases, prejudices, and triggers to foster an inclusive and supportive environment. By practicing mindfulness collectively, groups can establish a foundation of mutual understanding and empathy, allowing for healthier relationships and increased teamwork.

According to Atkins and Parker's research [15], compassionate organizational behavior is positively associated with more helpful behavior, heightened trust, support, and cooperation. They contended that compassionate behavior necessitates a regulated response that involves cognition, rather than an automatic reaction. Furthermore, they postulated that mindfulness may serve as a crucial enabler of compassionate behavior, affording employees the capacity to respond consciously to situations, rather than react automatically.

Furthermore, mindfulness cultivates a culture of respect by encouraging individuals to actively listen to one another, seek common ground, and appreciate diverse perspectives. This open-minded approach helps to minimize misunderstandings and promote effective communication, ultimately leading to more successful conflict resolution.

6. Mindfulness and leadership

In recent years, companies have recognized the benefits of integrating mindfulness into their leadership practices. These organizations offer various resources, training programs, and workshops to cultivate mindfulness skills among leaders. The advantages of practicing mindful organizing are believed to yield both strategic and operational advantages by establishing feedback loops and communication channels between front-line employees and leadership to enhance organizational processes [16].

One key benefit of mindfulness in leadership is the development of self-awareness. Through practicing mindfulness, leaders can become more aware of their thoughts, emotions, and behaviors, enabling them to make conscious and informed decisions. This self-awareness also extends to their interactions with others, fostering better communication, empathy, and relationship-building skills. Mindfulness helps leaders to enhance their focus and attention, which is crucial in a fast-paced and complex business environment. By learning to be fully present in the moment, leaders improve their ability to prioritize tasks, manage time effectively, and make strategic decisions.

Reb et al.'s [17] study indicated a positive correlation between the trait mindfulness of leaders and various aspects of employee well-being and job performance. They posited that mindfulness enabled leaders to cultivate better connections with their subordinates and attune themselves to their needs, which resulted in improved job satisfaction and overall performance. Moreover, the benefits of mindfulness are not limited to leadership roles alone. Still, they can also extend to other domains involving interpersonal interaction, such as communication and negotiation [18, 19].

These organizations also emphasize the importance of mindfulness in promoting well-being, resilience, and stress management among leaders. By incorporating mindfulness practices into their daily routines, leaders can reduce burnout, enhance.

6.1 Effects of mindful leader on organization conflicts

A mindful leader can actively work to decline conflict in the workplace. As previously mentioned, mindfulness involves being fully present in the moment and awareness of one's thoughts and the environment. By practicing mindfulness and developing emotional intelligence, a leader can be more attentive to potential conflicts and take steps to prevent or de-escalate them. By being mindful and employing these strategies, a leader can create a more harmonious and productive work environment, reducing the likelihood of conflict.

One such leader is Nelson Mandela, who demonstrated outstanding leadership during his time as the President of South Africa. He showed compassion, forgiveness, and strong determination, which not only united his divided nation but also inspired the world. Another example is Jeff Bezos, the founder of Amazon. Bezos had a clear vision for his company and the determination to turn it into a reality. He also emphasized customer-centricity and innovation, which played a crucial role in shaping Amazon into the e-commerce giant that it is today.

Here are some ways a mindful leader can decline conflict in the workplace:

1. Open Communication: Foster an environment of open and honest communication where employees feel comfortable discussing concerns, issues, and differences.

2. Active Listening: Practice active listening skills, showing genuine interest in other's perspectives and opinions. It creates a sense of trust and helps prevent misunderstandings.

3. Clear Roles and Expectations: Clearly define roles, responsibilities, and expectations for all team members, providing a clear framework for everyone to Collaborate. It promotes a collaborative working culture that emphasizes teamwork and cooperative problem-solving, leading to the decline of competition and conflict.

4. Conflict Resolution Skills: Develop conflict resolution skills and encourage employees to do the same. Provide training or resources to help employees effectively manage and resolve conflicts.

5. Emotional Intelligence: Develop emotional intelligence to understand and manage emotions in oneself and others. It allows for better empathy, understanding, and communication during conflicts.

6. Address Issues Proactively: Address potential sources of concerns that might arise and take action to prevent them from escalating.

7. Lead by Example: Model positive behaviors and conflict resolution strategies as a leader. Demonstrate good communication, empathy, and fairness in your own interactions.

8. Building trust: Mindful leaders prioritize building trust among team members. By creating a psychologically safe environment, they encourage open and honest communication. When employees trust their leader and feel safe expressing their opinions and concerns, conflicts are less likely to occur or escalate.

9. Fostering a positive work culture: Mindful leaders actively work toward fostering a positive work culture that values teamwork, appreciation, and inclusivity. Promoting a sense of belonging and shared purpose creates an environment where conflicts are less likely to arise, and employees feel motivated to work together harmoniously.

7. Real-world organizations that have successfully implemented mindfulness programs

One example of a real-world organization that has successfully implemented mindfulness programs to decline conflict is Google. In recent years, Google has made mindfulness a central focus of their employee well-being initiatives. Google's most popular mindfulness course, "Search Inside Yourself," offered since 2007, trains employees in mindfulness practices such as meditation and self-awareness.

By implementing this program, Google has seen positive results in reducing conflict and improving employee well-being. Google believes that these mindfulness programs teach emotional intelligence, which helps people better understand their colleagues' motivations.

Another example is Aetna, an American health insurance company. Aetna introduced mindfulness programs as part of their employee wellness initiatives to address workplace stress and improve overall. Aetna developed, launched, and studied two mindfulness programs in 2010—Viniyoga Stress Reduction and Mindfulness at Work—in collaboration with Duke University, eMindful, and the American Viniyoga Institute. The goals of the programs were to help reduce stress and to improve reactions to stress. Participants in both programs showed significant improvement in perceived stress levels and productivity of employers.

General Mills has offered mindfulness programs to its employees in its Minneapolis headquarters since 2006. The courses are designed to improve employee focus, clarity, and creativity. The company also offers weekly meditation sessions and yoga classes, and it has a dedicated meditation room in every building on its campus.

Intel began offering its Awake@Intel mindfulness program in 2012. On average, participants report a two-point decrease (on a scale of 1 to 10) in stress and feeling overwhelmed, a three-point increase in overall happiness and well-being, and a two-point increase in new ideas, insights, mental clarity, creativity, ability to focus, quality of relationships at work, and level of engagement in meetings, projects, and team efforts—all articulated goals of the program.

Green Mountain Coffee Roasters has also embraced mindfulness. The company offers monthly daylong mindfulness retreats to its employees, their families, and friends.

It is unsurprising that AstraZeneca has incorporated mindfulness techniques to alleviate employee stress consequent to being compelled to deliver outcomes in the course of the Covid-19 pandemic. AstraZeneca has been at the forefront of ensuring global safety and the return to normalcy; however, their personnel have been equally affected by the psychological strains of the lockdown. Indeed, AstraZeneca has published a dedicated employee wellbeing handbook to steer staff members through the transitioning process of returning to work after the pandemic. The guidebook set out methods to manage physical and mental wellbeing, including mindfulness as a fundamental technique to enhance mental health [20].

Nike has an outstanding history of encouraging a healthy work environment. Nike was one of the first businesses to provide their employees with weekly free meditation classes and free yoga—the activity has since expanded to many more of their locations across the world. By promoting mindfulness, Nike allows its employees to feel refreshed and focused while on the job, resulting in improved work performance and a decrease in sick days.

Bjorn Anderson, Recruiting Manager at Nike said about the program:

It can be easy to focus so much on physical activity for the body that sometimes we forget to exercise the mind. Nike is committed to our total wellness. I started meditating almost 2 years ago (thanks to my wife). Meditation has transformed my life both personally and professionally, in only 3 minutes or less per day [21].

8. Conflicts can facilitate change and progress

While mindfulness can contribute significantly to declining conflict in the workplace, it's important to note that conflict is a natural part of human interactions. On some occasions, it can lead to positive outcomes such as increased levels of innovation, improved decision-making processes, and the strengthening of social connections.

When individuals have different viewpoints or ideas, it can give rise to innovative solutions. Conflicts challenging existing norms or ideas foster a culture of thinking outside the box, pushing individuals to explore alternative approaches. Conflicts have the potential to enhance decision-making processes. Introducing Diverse viewpoints contributes to more comprehensive discussions and the analysis of various alternatives. This can ultimately lead to improved decisions by considering different perspectives and potential consequences. Conflicts can strengthen relationships. When conflicts are approached with open-mindedness and a willingness to understand others, they allow individuals to communicate and collaborate more effectively. Conflicts can lead to greater mutual understanding and respect through constructive dialog and compromise.

While conflicts are generally seen as harmful and disruptive, they can also have positive outcomes when managed effectively. It is important to note that a mindful leader can manage conflicts effectively to harness their potential for positive change. Leaders need to create a safe and supportive environment for conflict resolution, encourage respectful dialog, and facilitate productive discussions. By doing so, conflicts can become catalysts for growth, innovation, and progress in the workplace. Here are some ways conflicts can contribute to positive change by considering the mindfulness approach.

8.1 Non-judgmental approach

Conflicts often arise when a team or organization has underlying issues or problems. These conflicts can act as a signal that something needs attention or improvement. By addressing the root causes of conflicts, leaders can identify and resolve underlying problems, leading to positive changes in processes, systems, or team dynamics.

Mindful leaders approach conflicts without judgment or bias, and create an atmosphere where individuals feel safe expressing their opinions and concerns without fear of being criticized or dismissed. By suspending judgment, they encourage open dialog and help individuals explore the underlying causes of the conflict.

8.2 Active listening and empathy

Conflict resolution processes often involve open and honest communication, active listening, and finding common ground. Through these processes, individuals can develop stronger relationships built on trust, understanding, and respect. Resolving conflicts can create a foundation for better collaboration, teamwork, and a more positive work environment.

Mindful leaders practice active listening, paying full attention to the perspectives and concerns of all parties involved in the conflict. They demonstrate empathy by understanding and acknowledging the emotions and needs of each individual. By showing genuine interest and empathy, they can foster understanding and collaboration.

They can facilitate constructive conversations, encouraging individuals to express themselves openly and honestly. They guide the discussion toward finding mutually beneficial solutions and work with the parties involved to reach agreements that address the root causes of the conflict.

8.3 Emotional self-regulation

Mindful leaders develop a strong sense of self-awareness, including an understanding of their emotions, triggers, and reactivity patterns. When conflicts arise, they remain calm, composed, and non-reactive, allowing them to approach the situation clearly and objectively. They can create a safe space for open dialog and problem-solving by managing their emotions. Mindful leaders can engage in the practice of non-reactivity, whereby they possess the ability to meticulously observe their emotions without rushing to act upon them. This skill enables them to create a distance between their emotions and their responses, enabling them to make conscious choices rather than being solely driven by their emotions.

When they face conflict or challenging situations, they can pause before responding. They use this time to reflect on their emotions, considering the potential impact of their actions and words. By taking this moment of reflection, they can respond more thoughtfully and constructively.

9. Conclusion

Mindfulness, rooted in Buddhist, is the practice of paying deliberate, non-judgmental attention to the present moment. By embracing mindfulness, we can achieve greater clarity, tranquility, and a stronger connection to ourselves and our surroundings. This practice empowers us to observe our thoughts, emotions, and sensations without being controlled by them, enabling us to respond consciously rather than react reflexively.

Introducing mindfulness into workplaces yields multifaceted benefits. It is not only a moral responsibility to prioritize the wellbeing of employees but also a strategic move with positive commercial outcomes. Workplace mindfulness can lead to reduced stress levels, lower turnover rates, heightened productivity, enhanced recruitment of top talent, and increased innovation.

Mindfulness operates on both individual and organizational levels. Individual mindfulness involves key aspects such as observation, awareness, and non-reactive acceptance of experiences. Organizational mindfulness, on the other hand, encompasses an unwavering focus on failures, a nuanced understanding of operations, resilience, and respect for expertise. Organizational mindfulness aids in recognizing potential threats early and responding effectively, fostering proactive problem-solving and innovative thinking.

In today's rapidly changing workplaces, marked by fast-paced environments and reactive tendencies, mindfulness takes on an essential role. The constant influx of information and demands can lead to impulsivity and stress, which hinder conflict resolution and overall wellbeing. Mindfulness provides a counterbalance by encouraging intentional responses over reactive behaviors. It empowers individuals to manage stress and approach conflicts with a clear mind, leading to more effective conflict resolution. Moreover, a culture of mindfulness at the workplace fosters open communication, empathy, and collaboration. In the midst of a world driven by urgency, mindfulness offers a path to effective conflict resolution, improved decision-making, successful negotiation, and enhanced wellbeing.

Negotiation effectiveness plays a pivotal role in conflict resolution, encompassing various factors such as mindfulness, emotional intelligence, and negotiation styles. Successful negotiators combine compromising, integrating, and dominating styles, while those with high emotional intelligence excel in understanding opponent's interests and emotions. Mindfulness, with its focus on openness, awareness, and emotional regulation, contributes positively to negotiation outcomes.

Mindfulness also enhances problem-solving skills by promoting non-judgmental awareness of the present moment. This state of mind reduces cognitive and emotional disruptions, allowing individuals to concentrate better and approach problems with clarity and creativity. Research supports that mindfulness improves cognitive flexibility, working memory, and emotional regulation, all critical for effective problem-solving.

Moreover, mindfulness positively influences decision-making processes. By aiding in the observation of events, mindfulness enhances objective decision-making. It helps manage information overload, mitigate cognitive rigidity, and reduce emotional biases. It also encourages the acknowledgment of mistakes and promotes learning from experiences, fostering resilience and courage in decision-makers. Ultimately, incorporating mindfulness into negotiation, problem-solving, and decision-making processes can lead to improved outcomes, better conflict resolution, and a more effective approach to challenges.

Fostering a culture of respect and compassion through mindfulness is a powerful approach to conflict resolution in both organizational and personal contexts. By cultivating mindfulness, individuals can break free from automatic reactions, manage biases, and create an inclusive and supportive environment.

In organizational settings, mindful leadership plays a pivotal role in conflict management and prevention. Leaders who practice mindfulness promote open dialog, active listening, and empathy, leading to improved relationships and better conflict resolution outcomes. Moreover, mindfulness programs implemented by real-world organizations such as Google, Aetna, and General Mills have showcased the positive impact of mindfulness on reducing conflict, enhancing well-being, and boosting overall performance.

However, it is important to recognize that conflicts can be catalysts for positive change when managed mindfully. Mindful leaders approach conflicts with a non-judgmental perspective, actively listen to all parties involved, and regulate their emotions. By addressing underlying issues and fostering open communication, conflicts can lead to innovation, improved decision-making and strengthened relationships.

In a world where conflicts are inevitable, mindfulness offers a pathway to resolving disputes in a respectful, compassionate, and productive manner. By cultivating mindfulness individually and collectively, individuals and organizations can transform conflicts into opportunities for growth, collaboration, and positive transformation.

Author details

Zohreh Hosseinzadeh
Tehran University, Tehran, Iran

*Address all correspondence to: hosseinzadeh.zohreh@gmail.com

References

[1] Kay AA, Skarlicki DP. Cultivating a conflict-positive workplace: How mindfulness facilitates constructive conflict management. Organizational Behavior and Human Decision Processes. 2020;**159**:8-20. DOI: 10.1016/j.obhdp.2020.02.005

[2] Hülsheger UR, Alberts HJ, Feinholdt A, Lang JW. Benefits of mindfulness at work: The role of mindfulness in emotion regulation, emotional exhaustion, and job satisfaction. Journal of Applied Psychology. 2013;**98**:310. DOI: 10.1037/a0031313

[3] Kabat-Zinn J. Handbook of Where You Go, There You Are: Mindfulness Meditation in Everyday Life. London: Piatkus; 1994. p. 4

[4] Vogus TJ, Welbourne TM. Structuring for high reliability: HR practices and mindful processes in reliability-seeking organizations. Journal of Organizational Behavior. 2003;**24**:877-903. DOI: 10.1002/job.221

[5] Kelemen P, Born E, Ondráček T. Theorizing on the connection between organizational and individual mindfulness. Economic Research-Ekonomska Istraživanja. 2020;**33**:1813-1829. DOI: 10.3390/su132413852

[6] Pérez-Yus MC, Ayllón-Negrillo E, Delsignore G, Magallón-Botaya R, Aguilar-Latorre A, Oliván Blázquez B. Variables associated with negotiation effectiveness: The role of mindfulness. Frontiers in Psychology. 2020;**11**:1214. DOI: 10.3389/fpsyg.2020.01214

[7] Reb J, Narayanan J, Chaturvedi S. Leading mindfully: Two studies on the influence of supervisor trait mindfulness on employee well-being and performance. Mindfulness. 2014;**5**:36, 45. DOI: 10.1007/s12671-012-0144-z

[8] D'Zurilla TJ, Nezu AM. Problem-solving therapies. In: Dobson KS, editor. Handbook of Cognitive–Behavioral Therapies. New York: Guilford Press; 2001. pp. 211-245

[9] Ren J, Huang Z, Luo J, Wei G, Ying X, Ding Z, et al. Meditation promotes insightful problem-solving by keeping people in a mindful and alert conscious state. Science China Life Sciences. 2011;**54**:961-965. DOI: 10.1007/s11427-011-4233-3

[10] Ostafin BD, Kassman KT. Stepping out of history: Mindfulness improves insight problem solving. Consciousness and Cognition. 2012;**21**:1031-1036. DOI: 10.1016/j.concog.2012.02.014

[11] Bajaj B, Khoury B, Sengupta S. Resilience and stress as mediators in the relationship of mindfulness and happiness. Frontiers in Psychology. 2022;**13**:771263. DOI: 10.3389/fpsyg.2022.771263

[12] Greenberg J, Reiner K, Meiran N. Mind the trap: Mindfulness practice reduces cognitive rigidity. PLoS One. 2012;**7**(5):e36206. DOI: 10.1371/journal.pone.0036206

[13] Gesell N, Niklas F, Schmiedeler S, Segerer R. Mindfulness and romantic relationship outcomes: The mediating role of conflict resolution styles and closeness. Mindfulness. 2020;**11**:2314-2324. DOI: 10.1007/s12671-020-01449-9

[14] Karelaia N. Why mindful individuals make better decisions. In: Howells C, editor. France: Insead; 2014. Available

from: http://knowledge.insead.edu [Accessed: July 23, 2014]

[15] Atkins PW, Parker SK. Understanding individual compassion in organizations: The role of appraisals and psychological flexibility. Academy of Management Review. 2012;**37**:524-546. DOI: 10.5465/amr.2010.0490

[16] Vogus TJ, Sutcliffe KM. Organizational mindfulness and mindful organizing: A reconciliation and path forward. Academy of Management Learning & Education. 2012;**11**:722-735. DOI: 10.5465/amle.2011.0002c

[17] Reb J, Chaturvedi S, Narayanan J, Kudesia RS. Leader mindfulness and employee performance: A sequential mediation model of LMX quality, interpersonal justice, and employee stress. Journal of Business Ethics. 2019;**160**:745-763. DOI: 10.1007/s10551-018-3927-x

[18] Block-Lerner J, Adair C, Plumb JC, Rhatigan DL, Orsillo SM. The case for mindfulness-based approaches in the cultivation of empathy: Does nonjudgmental, present-moment awareness increase capacity for perspective-taking and empathic concern? Journal of Marital and Family Therapy. 2007;**33**:501-516. DOI: 10.1111/j.1752-0606.2007.00034.x

[19] Wachs K, Cordova JV. Mindful relating: Exploring mindfulness and emotion repertoires in intimate relationships. Journal of Marital and Family Therapy. 2007;**33**:464-481. DOI: 10.1111/j.1752-0606.2007.00032.x

[20] 9 Mindful Businesses: Big companies that practice mindfulness [Internet]. 2022. Available from: https://yoursapp.com/business/blog/mindful-businesses/ [Accessed: July 27, 2022]

[21] Kimberly S. Why Google, Target, and General Mills Are Investing in Mindfulness [Internet]. 2015. Available from: https://hbr.org/2015/12/why-google-target-and-general-mills-are-investing-in-mindfulness [Accessed: December 28, 2015]

Chapter 7

Technology Self-Efficacy and Mindfulness as Coping Strategies for Technostress in Hybrid Work Settings

Martha Harunavamwe and Herbert Kanengoni

Abstract

Information technology (IT) has brought a number of benefits in aiding remote work and facilitating hybrid work models. Though individuals are enjoying the benefits, hybrid work settings are characterised by ambiguity and excessive use of technology, which may result in technostress and may influence well-being negatively. Within this hybrid work model, a number of techno-stressors may impede employee efficiency and trigger anxiety. Among the stressors are techno-overload, techno-complexity, techno-unreliability, techno-uncertainty and techno-invasion. These techno-stressors may be exacerbated by other hybrid work model challenges including long working hours, consistent connectivity, emotional exhaustion, demand for higher cognitive abilities, workaholism and overload. Technostress has thus emerged as a critical issue within the realm of management, owing to its propensity to impose pronounced repercussions on employee welfare and work-life equilibrium, in ways that can significantly impact the overall efficiency of organisations. This chapter contributes and expands literature by identifying technology self-efficacy and mindfulness as coping mechanisms that can be applied by organisations to mitigate the negative consequences of techno-stressors. The recommendations offer practical value in developing, planning and implementing targeted interventions that enable individuals to cope. Practising and implementing technology self-efficacy and mindfulness strategies can protect employees from the negative consequences of technostress, enhance well-being and improve the overall performance of the organisation.

Keywords: technology self-efficacy, mindfulness, coping strategies, technostress, hybrid work settings

1. Introduction

A recent survey revealed that nine out of ten employees expect flexibility at work and they are ready to quit if they do not get it [1]. In response, about 77% of organisations have opted for hybrid work settings. Thus, understanding the changing working landscape and providing physical spaces that revolutionise innovation and provide the technology needed to enable the hybrid work facets have become crucial. Additionally, the proliferation of IT to facilitate hybrid work settings within organisations has resulted in significant alterations, enhancements and heightened effectiveness. Nonetheless, there exist unfavourable facets linked to the stress induced by IT [2, 3]. This phenomenon, known as 'technostress', denotes the stress encountered by employees due to the extended and intensive utilisation of IT. Unforeseen technology slowdowns or breakdowns, as well as unfamiliarity with software, applications and technology, can result in employee stress leading to feelings of anxiety and hopelessness in technology-dependent industries [4, 5]. The impacts of technostress are substantial, with projections indicating that its repercussions incur a financial toll exceeding 100 billion pounds annually for businesses in the United Kingdom. This stems from diminished workforce productivity, elevated rates of employee absenteeism, heightened turnover and escalated expenditures on insurance [6].

Considering the evident influence of technostress on corporate performance and its potential implications for the overarching prosperity of organisations, it becomes imperative to strategize interventions within the evolving paradigm of hybrid work settings to ameliorate the effects of technostress. Organisational mechanisms known as technostress inhibitors, such as literacy enhancement, frequent technical assistance, and engagement facilitation, have been applied commonly as strategies to effectively diminish the influence of technostress on employees [7]. However, with the shift to a hybrid work model, the problem seems to have taken a new turn and presents unique challenges [8, 9]. Only limited research has explored alternative methods of alleviating the adverse impacts of technostress within the hybrid model. Research has suggested that leveraging personal resources, such as technology self-efficacy [10], and mindfulness can act as potential mechanisms to alleviate technostress and hybrid work challenges [6]. Although previous studies have investigated extensively the beneficial effects of personal resources on work-related stress in general [11, 12], we examine the role of technology self-efficacy and mindfulness both to mitigate the effects of technostress and to alleviate its negative consequences. This chapter tries to answer the question: how can these two personal resources (technology self-efficacy and mindfulness) be applied as coping strategies for technostress creators within the hybrid work setting? The following sections will be addressed in the chapter: an outline of the challenges associated with technology in hybrid work models, technostress creators, other challenges of hybrid work models, theoretical explanations, personal resources, technology self-efficacy, mindfulness, practical tips, lessons learnt and recommendations.

2. Challenges associated with technology use in hybrid work environments: techno-stressors

Technostress has been referred to as a modern disease of adaptation, a condition resulting from the difficulty of adapting to new IT [13]. No one is spared from the pace at which technology is changing and improving. Individuals are attempting to handle the constantly altering and developing information and communication technologies (ICTs), which introduce novel complexities in adapting to the frequent transformations in the cognitive, social and physical demands imposed by ICT within work contexts [14]. The prevalent adoption of virtual and hybrid work arrangements facilitated by ICT has engendered a series of stress-inducing factors for employees, encompassing issues such as excessive workload, encroachment on personal time, unclear role

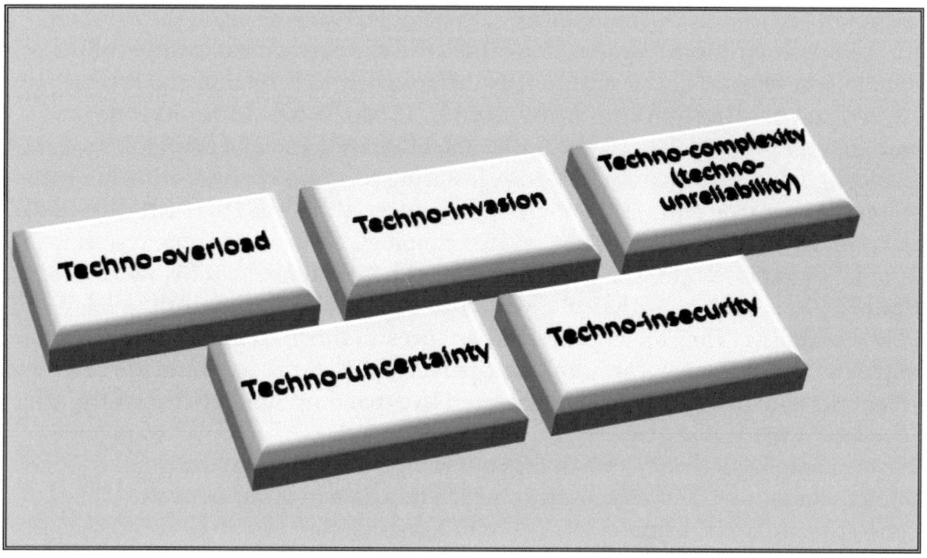

Figure 1.
Technostress creators.

expectations, intricate demands and heightened job insecurity [15]. Research has indicated that some individuals may experience anxiety, fear and stress when they perceive a lack of competence in utilising new devices, applications and software effectively, and adapting to, or coping with new ICTs in their work [14, 16]. Within the hybrid work model, the technostress challenges are exacerbated by constant adoption of new company systems, new software and the excessive and simultaneous use of multiple devices (laptops, tablets, cell phones) [16, 17]. Ragu-Nathan et al. [18] have identified and classified five technostress creators experienced by employees, including techno-complexity, techno-overload, techno-insecurity, techno-invasion and techno-uncertainty. The techno-stressors are illustrated in **Figure 1**.

2.1 Technostress creators

Techno-overload is one of the major challenges imposed on employees by the hybrid work setting. Techno-overload is experienced when work with digital technologies is demanding because of a high pace, frequent interruptions, multitasking, prolonged working time, expectations with regard to response times in digital communication. Employees being forced both to multitask and to execute their duties at a high speed [19]. The amount of information that individuals have to absorb from ICTs can be massive and difficulty to comprehend, to the extent that it results in adverse consequences and harmful impacts on individual health. A good example is that, within hybrid work environments, the practice of staying connected with the central office through the use of a variety of devices (such as laptops, phones, emails and instant messaging), along with engaging in diverse job tasks, reduce the quality of work and decrease effectiveness of tasks. This decline occurs because the employee's cognitive processing demands sufficient time to effectively assimilate the acquired information [20].

Closely associated with techno-overload is *techno-complexity*, referring to the high complexities presented by new ICTs which cause an employee to feel incompetent [21]. Increased complexity in both devices and software elicits high levels of frustration and diminishes individuals' psychological well-being, as they grapple with the cognitive effort required to comprehend the operational nuances of the technological system. This results in frustration, poor performance and low productivity and negatively affects well-being [22]. These complexities also trigger *techno-uncertainty*, which is a constant feeling of uncertainty and ambiguity caused by chronic digital transformation processes fostering constant change owing to upgrades in computer hardware and software [23]. The uncertainty leads to frustration and a perceived inability to cope with the rapid technological advancements, resulting in a fear of being replaced [19]. This is associated with *techno-unreliability*, which is stress induced by breakdowns, technical errors, load shedding, poor network, weak Wi-Fi and low usability. When an employee experiences all three: techno-overload, techno-complexity and techno-uncertainty, they perceive their work environment to be both challenging and ambiguous; hence, the need to expand resources to buffer the effects of overload and complexity.

If the complex demands and ambiguous environment are not managed well, this may also result in feelings of insecurity which translate to *techno-insecurity*. Thus, techno-insecurity is the fear of job loss or of a degradation in status caused by the perception that digital technologies or more qualified personnel will fully or partially replace one's own job/position [24]. The constant feeling of being overwhelmed with technology change threatens job security and makes employees feel that they may be replaced by new information systems or by better equipped or more technologically skilled employees [25]. Instead of focusing on producing good results, employees frequently spend much of their time experiencing fear of job loss owing to automation. In addition, within the hybrid work settings, employees operate from both home and office and this may pose challenges related to another techno-stressor referred to as techno-invasion. This phenomenon denotes the intrusion of (ICTs) into an employee's personal life, making it hard to separate work from private time, thus blurring the boundaries between professional and private spheres [26]. Hybrid environments enable high flexibility, which can blur boundaries between work and other life domains, causing work-life conflicts and impairing recovery from work. Mahapatra and Pati [27] found techno-invasion to be related negatively to well-being in employees. When employees are exposed to elevated levels of technostress, they eventually suffer the psychological strains of diminished commitment, struggle to flourish and display signs of languishing [28], have poor self-esteem [29] and show dissatisfaction with the IT system [20], and burnout [30]. It is clear that the adverse impacts of technostress are not limited to behavioural manifestations only such as diminished performance, high absenteeism and poor productivity, but also manifest in psychological ways including, anxiety, low organisational commitment, depression and low morale [28, 31].

2.2 Other challenges of hybrid work model

Besides the challenges related to technostress identified in the previous section, other negative effects of hybrid work include extended work hours, constant accessibility, emotional drain, need for greater thinking skills, excessive dedication to work, overwhelming tasks, overload and health problems affecting, for instance, the musculoskeletal system [32–34]. The hybrid work model also upsets work-life balance through blurring the boundaries between work and personal life, the extension of working hours and the intensification of work, including e-mail activity, in particular [32]. The ambiguity between professional and private time create conflicts that negatively affects well-being, disrupt the work-life integration, cause exhaustion and negatively impact individual productivity [33]. The minimised face-to-face interactions intensify the challenges of social, psychological and emotional relationships. All of these stressors require unique interventions that are designed to empower individuals to cope with challenges. In this regard, it is important to reflect on theory.

3. Theoretical explanations (JD-R model and TAM)

Some of the challenges caused by technostress in the hybrid work setting are a result of the failure of individuals to accept technology, the inability to use the software or systems of some devices as well as negative attitudes towards the usefulness of these technologies. In line with the technology acceptance model (TAM), individuals who use technology are driven by three key factors: their perception of the technology's usefulness, their perception of how easy it is to use and their overall attitude towards using it. This attitude is notably shaped by their perception of the technology's usefulness and its ease of use [35]. When employees struggle to use IT, they perceive themselves as incompetent and experience techno-insecurity. These perceptions of incompetence increase technostress levels and diminish productivity [28, 36]. Studies show that low-level individual ability, such as ICT literacy, positively predict high technostress [37], and that self-efficacy plays a role in shaping positive perceptions towards the use of technology. Yahşi and Hopcan [38] determined that high self-efficacy predicts low technostress. TAM3 offers a comprehensive list of interventions that have direct implications for decision-making regarding IT implementation and management [39]. Among these interventions is computer self-efficacy, which contributes significantly to perceived ease of use. The perception of competence in technology is a major factor in technostress and determines the attitude towards technology. When an individual's required technological competence exceeds their current abilities, the demands are perceived to be high and stress occurs [38]. In such cases, individuals rely on personal resources such as technology self-efficacy to deal with the challenges.

Based on the Job Demands Resource model (JD-R model) [40] and from the perspective of the conservation of resource theory (COR) [41], increasing resources may help to buffer the effects of high job demands and job stressors. Thus, we theorise that with adequate resources (e.g. personal resources; mindfulness and technology self-efficacy), even when exposed to technostress creators, employees are more likely to thrive in hybrid work models. Considering that the hybrid work space is characterised by technical failures, unfamiliar software, new devices, defective functionalities or long waiting times, it can easily be a source of frustration, with stress imposing high job demands on employees. Consistently being exposed to an environment with demands that exceed capabilities and resources to accomplish a task results in stress, burnout and eventually, low productivity. Both hybrid work setting and technostress expose employees to high job demands platforms. Fortunately, based on the COR theory, employees possess a range of resources (work and non-work) at their disposal, and these resources can be used to deal with the demands placed on them by their working environment. When employees invest in the development or use of resources, they synergistically combine different resources to cultivate additional reserves [42], and they flourish. When employees have an abundance of such resources, they create resource caravans to deal with all sorts of demands and stressors [41]. Typical stress reactions include anxiety, mental fatigue, scepticism and feelings of inefficiency, which call for the utilisation of more personal resources than job resources to buffer the effects of technostress and to maintain productivity. Therefore, training individuals to utilise their personal resources, such as self-efficacy and mindfulness, can typically aid as coping mechanisms within high techno-stressful environments. The experience of technostress is highly individual and the utilisation of personal resources could be of great assistance especially for hybrid work settings.

4. Personal resources: coping with technostress in hybrid work settings

The noted technostress creators and the challenges imposed by the hybrid work setting have psychological impacts on employees. They are linked, among other things, to reduced well-being and intensified stress [43]. The hybrid model holds appeal due to its potential to blend the advantages of office-based work, including opportunities for collaboration, innovation and in-person interactions with colleagues, with the added flexibility associated with working from home. While beneficial to both employees and organisations, as noted above, it has some downsides. In a comparative analysis of employees operating under three distinct work models (remote, hybrid and stationary) [44], results indicated that individual groups differed in terms of resource gains and resource losses based on the work environment. Relatively, the group that experienced both the strongest losses and strongest gains of resources globally and in most specific areas were the hybrid workers. From a long-term perspective, this suggests that working within the hybrid model, compared to the other models, can generate the strongest changes (both positive and negative) in different areas of life. This implies that, although empirical reports to date have mainly emphasised the positive consequences of hybrid work [45], in practice the hybrid work model may also be accompanied by a number of negative effects if employees do not have access to the required psychosocial resources.

It is clear that, since hybrid models have sparked a new wave of experimentation, this will undoubtedly become an increasingly common experience for many individuals and organisations. Companies are implementing different solutions and approaches to find out what works best for both employees and the business [38]. Reflecting on the elements of the Job Demands Resource model, technostress and hybrid work settings are seen as difficult job demands imposed on employees, and technology self-efficacy and mindfulness are seen as personal resources that employees may use to buffer the effects of those job demands. Thus, nurturing, investing and accumulating personal resources for hybrid employees may impact positively on how they deal with the challenges and demands associated with both technostress and hybrid environments in the long term. For example, a combination of technology self-efficacy and mindfulness techniques can reduce employee stress and burnout and can improve employee well-being [12]. What follows is a discussion of how technology self-efficacy and mindfulness can be used to aid challenges related to technostress and hybrid work settings.

4.1 Technology self-efficacy as a coping strategy

Self-efficacy is based on Bandura's social learning theory, and it is viewed as the adaptation and change in the behaviours of individuals according to their environment [46]. High levels of self-efficacy assist individuals in being confident, consciously determined and fulfilling their responsibilities in those domains where they have self-efficacy [47]. It is also positively related to active problem-focused coping, and negatively related to vital exhaustion and anxiety [48], which are caused by technostress. This chapter will focus on domain-specific self-efficacy (computer/technology self-efficacy). This is referred to as person's estimation of their ability to use technological devices/systems to complete work tasks [49]. Individuals with good technology self-efficacy and proper guidelines learn fast and adjust better in hybrid work models [50]. Studies have indicated [5] that technology self-efficacy has a significant relationship with technostress and that it moderates the relationship between technostress and workload. Technology self-efficacy reduces the perceived technostress through influencing thinking processes and biases towards technology use, and it regulates how people anticipate the use of technology [51]. Some studies note that technological self-efficacy and technical support reduces perceived stress through positively manipulating individual perceptions towards technology use [13, 15, 51]. Training self-efficacy is thus useful in controlling the technostress and maintaining the performance of employees. It has been observed that employees with greater computer self-efficacy experience reduced levels of computer-related technostress, while those with low technology self-efficacy and high technology dependence experience increased levels of computer-related technostress [46, 52]. Individuals who are high in technology self-efficacy are computer self-efficient, believe in themselves to solve problems relating to ICT, and eventually overcome techno-complexity and techno-uncertainty.

Hybrid work models are associated with demanding circumstances that have the potential to induce stress. In such instances, the abilities that aid individuals in managing their emotional responses and adjusting to the increasing pressures assume significance [53]. There is a need for adaptive functioning, which could help employees to experience a positive effect in negative situations. Circumstances like the exposure to negative conditions such as techno-overload and techno-complexity could end up with undesirable outcomes like anxiety and strain. One of the adaptive functioning skills mentioned could result from self-efficacy beliefs. Thus, the capacity to manage different negative conditions and emotions appropriately rests on different abilities and self-efficacy beliefs [53]. Self-efficacy is the leverage that individuals depend on while dealing successfully with challenging situations. In this context, since the stress is triggered by ICTs, it is proposed that the domain-specific self-efficacy (technological self-efficacy) might act as a buffer to extenuate the effects of technostress. Literature has indicated that technology self-efficacy can play a positive role in the successful use of technology [37, 54]. Taking into consideration the fact that technostress represents individual responses to technology-based expectations, individuals who possess technology self-efficacy might be able to reduce their technostress levels.

4.2 Mindfulness as a coping strategy for technostress

Digitisation forces all employees to be tech-savvy but some employees struggle to adapt to new technology. It is important to explore the role of mindfulness as a potential alleviator to stress induced by extended IT usage. Mindfulness involves consciously bringing one's awareness to the present moment, with openness, curiosity and acceptance of both pleasant and unpleasant experiences [55]. The purposeful focusing of attention encourages awareness of our habitual mental functioning (the auto-pilot mode). There are different perspectives on mindfulness; for example, it is depicted as a state, a dispositional trait, an attitude, a type of meditation and an intervention programme [56]. To date, attention has been on dispositional mindfulness/trait mindfulness, which is malleable and can be enhanced and cultivated through training and interventions programmes [6]. Of more interest is the domain-specific mindfulness (IT mindfulness), which is oriented towards IT use and its contexts, and it is believed to reduce perceptions of technostress [11]. IT, mindfulness was first introduced through the work of Ramiller and Burton Swanson [57], which proposed the idea of incorporating it into the processes of IT innovation in an organisation. Related to this, in 2018, Thatcher et al [58] systematically developed the concept of IT mindfulness, defined as 'a dynamic IT-specific trait, evident only when an individual is working with IT'.

IT mindfulness consists of four dimensions that help to explain how it can be applied as a coping strategy to manage challenges imposed by hybrid work models and technostress. The first dimension is alertness to distinction, which refers to the extent that an IT-mindful individual understands the capabilities of IT applications and the context in which they will prove useful. This aspect can help individuals to deal with both techno-uncertainty and techno-complexity. The second IT-mindfulness dimension is awareness of multiple perspectives. This refers to the IT-mindful individual who is able to identify multiple uses of specific IT applications as well as to develop innovative solutions to emerging problems [58, 59]. Considering that one of the major techno-stressors relates to the complexity of IT and the use of multiple devices, software and applications, dimension two can provide coping strategies for individuals struggling with techno-overload, techno-complexity and techno-uncertainty. The third dimension relates to openness to novelty. This refers to the individual's willingness to explore more potential and novel applications of the deployed system and relates well to techno-uncertainty as well. Individuals who explore their company systems more often experience less techno-uncertainty. The final dimension is orientation in the present, which refers to the IT-mindful individual who is focused on the present moment and context and is thus able to adapt technologies to several different contexts [59]. This dimension can help individuals to cope with techno-invasion and avoid getting carried away. An individual with a high levels of IT mindfulness will exhibit a greater degree of flexibility and adaptability when confronted with unforeseen situations (techno-unreliability) and novel technological occurrences within their work environment, leading to heightened levels of end-user contentment [60]. Correspondingly, an individual displaying high IT mindfulness possesses the capacity to modify their responses and alter viewpoints based on the circumstances, thereby formulating inventive resolutions to address technological intricacies and instances of technology malfunction that necessitate a congruence between the utilised technology and the specific task being undertaken [58, 61]. Mindfulness can thus offer significant advantages in the hybrid work context, such as work resilience and enhancing performance [62], while also reducing the burden of technostress.

In general, mindfulness strengthens one's ability to deal with job-related tensions that can impact the physical, mental and emotional well-being negatively. The practice of mindfulness helps employees to reduce the effects of stress. It helps individuals to be more effective in a busy and hi tech dependent work environment. It reduces stress, increases focus and improves the ability to deal with technology-imposed challenges, both at work and at home. Technology is evolving rapidly, so focusing one's mind to handle challenges with confidence is necessary. Mindfulness reduces technostress, enhances focus and promotes well-being. **Table 1** displays practical tips for cultivating digital mindfulness and technology self-efficacy to overcome technostress.

Techno-stressors and hybrid challenges	Mindfulness techniques	Technology self-efficacy techniques
Techno-overload	Mindful notifications: disable notifications on your mobile, tablet and popups on laptop Single tasking, do not multitask (e.g. avoid attending to emails during virtual meetings) Remove distractions (uninstall unused apps) Digital detox: take mindful pauses	Apply mastery experience, Social persuasion (accept encouragement from others and organisational support)
Techno-complexity	Focus on understanding details of IT devices, *apps*, systems and software used by your company before using it. Be mindful of the state of your mind when consuming content using technology	Practise technology-based self-directed learning Increase technological learning motivation Find and interact with role models Try new devices, apps and systems
Techno-invasion	Practise mindful emailing Be mindful of taking short breaks: Digital fasting and tech free zones Create boundaries for meetings	Build a supportive system
Techno-uncertainty	Pay attention and focus on understanding details of IT devices, *apps*, systems and software used in the organisation before using it. Have mindful conversations about technology with colleagues	Practise technology-based self-directed learning Increase technological learning motivation Vicarious experiences of observing others Modelling experiences
Techno-insecurity	Mindfulness-based stress reduction (MBSR) Gratitude for technology: recognize positive aspects of technology	Vicarious experiences of observing others Modelling or participation in technological training Social persuasion (accept encouragement from others and organisational support)
Techno-unreliability (breakdowns, weak connectivity, load shedding	MBSR	Access sufficient computers, sufficient software licences, strong Wi-Fi Be positive

Table 1.
Practical tips: cultivating mindfulness and technology self-efficacy.

5. Lessons learnt, and key takeaways

The narrative above has combined mindfulness and technology self-efficacy as buffering the effects of technostress in the hybrid work settings. It has been proven that combining technical competence with present-moment awareness and acceptance assists in navigating technostress-prone environments, overcoming technology challenges and fostering a healthier relationship with technology. The following are some key takeaways:

1. Technology self-efficacy provides employees with the necessary skills and confidence to navigate and troubleshoot technological challenges imposed by the hybrid work setting. Consistently, mindfulness helps individuals to approach

technology-related challenges with a clear and focused mind. This enables individuals to leverage their technical competence while maintaining a calm and present mindset to solve problems and reduce technostress effectively. Therefore, combining mindfulness techniques with technology self-efficacy may aid in coping with technostress.

2. Mindfulness provides the principles of establishing healthy boundaries and regulating the use of technology consciously. Additionally, technology self-efficacy helps individuals to change their perspectives on stressful issues. Instead of allowing self-doubt to bother them when using new technology or new applications, individuals may be inspired to develop solutions that work better for them. Thus, combining mindfulness and technology self-efficacy can help individuals to develop a balanced approach to technology in which they optimise its benefits while reducing the negative impacts that can contribute to techno-overload, techno-complexity and techno-uncertainty.

3. The process of nurturing technology self-efficacy equips employees with confidence and the skills to navigate challenges related to technology, and when this is coupled with practising mindfulness it enhances resilience and facilitates adaptability in the face of technostress. Practising IT-mindfulness techniques can support one's technology self-efficacy, and increase creativity and innovation. Therefore, combining mindfulness and self-efficacy enables individuals to manage hybrid work challenges and to cope more effectively in technostress-prone environments.

4. Mindfulness allows heightened self-awareness, which assists employees to recognise early signs of technostress, such as anxiety, frustration and complexity. Such awareness assists employees to apply their technology self-efficacy skills proactively to address potential techno-stressors before they escalate.

6. Recommendations for organisations and individuals

Evidence suggests that dispositional IT mindfulness is a malleable trait that can be enhanced through relevant training programmes and interventions [55]. The discourse presented above substantiates the beneficial contribution of mindfulness within the workplace, fortifying the standpoint that corporations should imbue mindfulness practices into their organisational fabric. Noteworthy entities, such as Facebook, Google and Intel [63], have been offering tailored in-house mindfulness sessions for their employees. Thus, modern organisations can create their own mindfulness programmes aligned to their technical challenges and promote stress-reduction strategies. Additionally, organisations should support the mindful use of technology, which promotes positive re-appraisal of the situation and activates positive coping mechanisms, like social support and taking breaks. Hence, developing, introducing and integrating mindfulness practices into work routines to reduce technostress and overcome challenges should be prioritised. Developing policies aimed at promoting occasional digital detoxes will encourage individuals to disconnect from technology outside of work hours. The policies should also address guidelines for the appropriate use of technology, enhancing a better work-life balance and reducing techno-invasion.

Besides the provision of IT training and support, organisations should offer detailed training aimed at enhancing technology self-efficacy. These trainings may include skills-building initiatives and mentorship opportunities addressing common technology challenges, developing digital literacy, and exploring new devices, systems and apps. It is suggested that organisations should consider adding training on developing technology self-efficacy and mindfulness in their wellness initiatives.

They should put in place open communication channels for employees to share their experiences and challenges related to technology use. For those struggling more with technostress, consideration should be given to opening forums where employees can share applicable coping strategies, seek advice and provide mutual support in dealing with techno-unreliability and other technical challenges. A strong support network should be established with a dedicated and accessible IT team as well as role models for those struggling with understanding the devices, new systems or applications.

Lastly, it is important to create a supportive hybrid work environment. This may include deploying regular surveys to assess levels of employee technostress in order to identify any potential stressors before they become detrimental. The surveys should be coupled with feedback sessions to discuss possible coping strategies. During these sessions, experts may identify areas where technology self-efficacy and mindfulness strategies can be integrated. On a regular basis, the impact of implemented coping strategies should be tracked and, where necessary, adjusted and new, proven and tested coping strategies should be introduced. Policies, training programmes and resources should be implemented to better support employees in managing technostress effectively in hybrid work models.

7. Conclusions

This chapter has indicated that the popularly adapted hybrid work setting is made possible by the use of technology, thus the digital workplace is a fundamental component of the hybrid work environment. Companies that are in the process of digitising key areas are witnessing enhanced outcomes in terms of collaboration, teamwork, data security, productivity, customer experiences and the overarching financial performance. However, the work-life boundaries have been blurred and technology seems to have its dark side affecting some employees. There is need to reconfigure the digital workplace to support hybrid work behaviours that eliminate technostress. New software, new devices and extended screen time experienced in hybrid settings can impede creativity by inducing technostress, fatigue and negatively impacting mood. On a team level, hybrid settings lack co-presence and hinder psychological safety since there is no immediate help from colleagues in case an employee encounters a technical challenge or experience technostress forcing employees to rely on themselves. Technology self-efficacy and mindfulness interventions are powerful tools that can buffer the negative consequences of technostress, enhance well-being at work and increase individual outcomes. These personal resources can counterbalance technostress conditions and improve end-user performance and satisfaction.

Acknowledgements

Acknowledgments go to University of Pretoria: Department of Human Resource Management.

Conflict of interest

The authors declare no conflict of interest.

Author details

Martha Harunavamwe* and Herbert Kanengoni
Department of Human Resource Management, University of Pretoria, Pretoria, South Africa

*Address all correspondence to: martha.harunavamwe@up.ac.za

References

[1] Rahmani Z. [Internet] Organizations must accelerate their digitalization efforts in four key areas to ensure a thriving hybrid work environment. 2022. Available from: https://www.ey.com/en_se/workplace-of-the-future/how-can-technology-activate-your-hybrid-work-ecosystem

[2] Fischer T, Riedl R. Technostress research: a nurturing ground for measurement pluralism. Communications of the Association for Information Systems. 2017;**40**(1):17

[3] Tarafdar M, Tu Q, Ragu-Nathan BS, Ragu-Nathan TS. The impact of technostress on role stress and productivity. Journal of Management Information Systems. 2007;**24**(1):301-328

[4] Yener S, Arslan A, Kilinç S. The moderating roles of technological self-efficacy and time management in the technostress and employee performance relationship through burnout. Information Technology and People. 2021;**34**(7):1890-1919

[5] Ali SS, Kaur R, Khan S. Identification of innovative technology enablers and drone technology determinants adoption: A graph theory matrix analysis framework. Operations Management Research. 2023;**16**(1):830-852

[6] Ioannou A, Tussyadiah I, Marshan A. Dispositional mindfulness as an antecedent of privacy concerns: a protection motivation theory perspective. Psychology and Marketing. 2021;**38**(10):1766-1778

[7] Tarafdar M, Pullins EB, Ragu-Nathan TS. Technostress: negative effect on performance and possible mitigations. International Surgery Journal. 2015;**25**(2):103-132

[8] Dey BL, Al-Karaghouli W, Muhammad SS. Adoption, adaptation, use and impact of information systems during pandemic time and beyond: research and managerial implications. Information Systems Management. 2020;**37**(4):298-302

[9] Molino M, Ingusci E, Signore F, Manuti A, Giancaspro ML, Russo V, et al. Wellbeing costs of technology use during Covid-19 remote working: an investigation using the Italian translation of the technostress creators scale. Sustainability. 2020;**12**(15):5911

[10] Tarabay K. The impact of technostress on work engagement [Doctoral dissertation]. Beirut: Lebanese American University; 2021

[11] Ioannou A, Papazafeiropoulou A. Using IT mindfulness to mitigate the negative consequences of technostress. In: 23rd Americas Conference on Information Systems; Boston, MA; 2017

[12] Pflügner K, Maier C, Weitzel T. The direct and indirect influence of mindfulness on techno-stressors and job burnout: a quantitative study of white-collar workers. Computers in Human Behavior. 2021;**115**:106566

[13] Kim S, Lee J. The mediating effects of ego resilience on the relationship between professionalism perception and technostress of early childhood teachers. International Journal of Learning, Teaching and Educational Research. 2021;**20**(4):245-264

[14] Nimrod G. Changes in internet use when coping with stress: older adults during the COVID-19 pandemic. The American Journal of Geriatric Psychiatry. 2020;**28**(10):1020-1024

[15] Truța C, Maican CI, Cazan AM, Lixăndroiu RC, Dovleac L, Maican MA. Always connected@ work. Technostress and well-being with academics. Computers in Human Behavior. 2023;**143**:107675

[16] Harunavamwe M, Ward C. The influence of technostress, work–family conflict, and perceived organisational support on workplace flourishing amidst COVID-19. Frontiers in Psychiatry. 2022;**13**:921211

[17] Jena RK. Technostress in ICT enabled collaborative learning environment: an empirical study among Indian academician. Computers in Human Behavior. 2015;**51**:1116-1123

[18] Ragu-Nathan TS, Tarafdar M, Ragu-Nathan BS, Tu Q. The consequences of technostress for end users in organizations: conceptual development and empirical validation. Information Systems Research. 2008;**19**(4):417-433

[19] Tarafdar M, Tu Q, Ragu-Nathan TS, Ragu-Nathan BS. Crossing to the dark side: examining creators, outcomes, and inhibitors of technostress. Communications of the ACM. 2011;**54**(9):113-120

[20] Ingusci E, Signore F, Giancaspro ML, Manuti A, Molino M, Russo V, et al. Workload, techno overload, and behavioral stress during COVID-19 emergency: the role of job crafting in remote workers. Frontiers in Psychiatry. 2021;**12**:655148

[21] Barber LK, Santuzzi AM. Please respond ASAP: workplace tele pressure and employee recovery. Journal of Occupational Health Psychology. 2015;**20**(2):172

[22] Day A, Paquet S, Scott N, Hambley L. Perceived information and communication technology (ICT) demands on employee outcomes: the moderating effect of organizational ICT support. Journal of Occupational Health Psychology. 2012;**17**(4):473

[23] Hwang I, Cha O. Examining technostress creators and role stress as potential threats to employees' information security compliance. Computers in Human Behavior. 2018;**81**:282-293

[24] Dragano N, Lunau T. Technostress at work and mental health: concepts and research results. Current Opinion in Psychiatry. 2020;**33**(4):407-413

[25] Ibrahim H, Yusoff YM. User characteristics as antecedents of techno stress towards EHRM: from experts' views. Procedia - Social and Behavioral Sciences. 2015;**172**:134-141

[26] La Torre G, De Leonardis V, Chiappetta M. Technostress: how does it affect the productivity and life of an individual? Results of an observational study. Public Health. 2020;**189**:60-65

[27] Mahapatra M, Pati SP. Technostress creators and burnout: a job demands-resources perspective. In: Proceedings of the 2018 ACM SIGMIS Conference on Computers and People Research 2018. pp. 70-77

[28] Tarafdar M, Stich JF. Virtual work, technology and wellbeing. In: Wall T, Cooper CL, Brough P, editors. The SAGE Handbook of Organizational Wellbeing. London: SAGE; 2021. pp. 159-169

[29] Korzynski P, Rook C, Florent Treacy E, Kets de Vries M. The impact of self-esteem, conscientiousness and pseudo-personality on technostress. Internet Research. 2021;**31**(1):59-79

[30] Afifi TD, Basinger ED, Kam JA. The extended theoretical model of communal

coping: understanding the properties and functionality of communal coping. The Journal of Communication. 2020;**70**(3):424-446

[31] Ayyagari R, Grover V, Purvis R. Technostress: Technological antecedents and implications. MIS Quarterly. 2011;**35**(4):831-858

[32] Spagnoli P, Molino M, Molinaro D, Giancaspro ML, Manuti A, Ghislieri C. Workaholism and technostress during the COVID-19 emergency: the crucial role of the leaders on remote working. Frontiers in Psychology. 2020;**11**:620310

[33] Shifrin NV, Michel JS. Flexible work arrangements and employee health: a meta-analytic review. Work and Stress. 2022;**36**(1):60-85

[34] Vaziri H, Casper WJ, Wayne JH, Matthews RA. Changes to the work–family interface during the COVID-19 pandemic: examining predictors and implications using latent transition analysis. The Journal of Applied Psychology. 2020;**105**(10):1073

[35] Lin F, Fofanah SS, Liang D. Assessing citizen adoption of e-Government initiatives in Gambia: a validation of the technology acceptance model in information systems success. Government Information Quarterly. 2011;**28**(2):271-279

[36] Paul N, Glassman M. Relationship between internet self-efficacy and internet anxiety: A nuanced approach to understanding the connection. Australasian Journal of Educational Technology. 2017;**33**(4):147-165

[37] Salanova M, Llorens S, Cifre E. The dark side of technologies: technostress among users of information and communication technologies. International Journal of Psychology. 2013;**48**(3):422-436

[38] Yahşi Ö, Hopcan S. Reviewing the structural relationship among the technology leadership, technostress and technology acceptance of school administrators. Anemon Muş Alparslan Üniversitesi Sosyal Bilimler Dergisi. 2021;**9**(6):1781-1797

[39] Venkatesh V, Bala H. Technology acceptance model 3 and a research agenda on interventions. Decision Sciences. 2008;**39**(2):273-315

[40] Bakker AB, Demerouti E. The job demands-resources model: state of the art. Journal of Managerial Psychology. 2007;**22**(3):309-328

[41] Hobfoll SE. Conservation of resource caravans and engaged settings. Journal of Occupational and Organizational Psychology. 2011;**84**(1):116-122

[42] Harunavamwe M, Nel P, Van Zyl E. The influence of self-leadership strategies, psychological resources, and job embeddedness on work engagement in the banking industry. South Africa Journal of Psychology. 2020;**50**(4):507-519

[43] Zacher H, Rudolph CW. Big five traits as predictors of perceived stressfulness of the COVID-19 pandemic. Personality and Individual Differences. 2021;**175**:110694

[44] Stasiła-Sieradzka M, Sanecka EA, Turska E. Not so good hybrid work model? Resource losses and gains since the outbreak of the COVID-19 pandemic and job burnout among non-remote, hybrid, and remote employees. International Journal of Occupational Medicine and Environmental Health. 2023;**36**(2):229-249

[45] Wörtler B, Van Yperen NW, Barelds DP. Do individual differences in need strength moderate the

relations between basic psychological need satisfaction and organizational citizenship behavior. Motivation and Emotion. 2020;**44**:315-328

[46] Shu Q, Tu Q, Wang K. The impact of computer self-efficacy and technology dependence on computer-related technostress: a social cognitive theory perspective. International Journal of Human Computer Interaction. 2011;**27**(10):923-939

[47] Lunenburg FC. Self-efficacy in the workplace: implications for motivation and performance. International Journal of Business Administration and Management. 2011;**14**(1):1-6

[48] Romppel M, Herrmann-Lingen C, Wachter R, Edelmann F, Düngen HD, Pieske B, et al. A short form of the General Self-Efficacy Scale (GSE-6): Development, psychometric properties and validity in an intercultural non-clinical sample and a sample of patients at risk for heart failure. GMS Psychosocial Medicine. 2013;**10**:1-7

[49] Compeau DR, Higgins CA. Computer self-efficacy: Development of a measure and initial test. MIS Quarterly. 1995;**19**(2):189-211

[50] Guoyan S, Khaskheli A, Raza SA, Khan KA, Hakim F. Teachers' self-efficacy, mental well-being and continuance commitment of using learning management system during COVID-19 pandemic: A comparative study of Pakistan and Malaysia. Interactive Learning Environments. 2021:1-23

[51] Saleem F, Malik MI, Qureshi SS, Farid MF, Qamar S. Technostress and employee performance nexus during COVID-19: training and creative self-efficacy as moderators. Frontiers in Psychology. 2021;**12**:595119

[52] Saidy J, Garanti Z, Sadaka R. Technostress creators and job performance among frontliners: theorizing the moderating role of self-efficacy. Frontiers in Psychology. 2022;**13**:827027

[53] Caprara G, Vecchione M, Barbaranelli C, Alessandri G. Emotional stability and affective self–regulatory efficacy beliefs: proofs of integration between trait theory and social cognitive theory. European Journal of Personality. 2013;**27**(2):145-154

[54] Delpechitre D, Black HG, Farrish J. The dark side of technology: examining the impact of technology overload on salespeople. The Journal of Business and Industrial Marketing. 2018;**34**(2):317-337

[55] Quaglia JT, Braun SE, Freeman SP, McDaniel MA, Brown KW. Meta-analytic evidence for effects of mindfulness training on dimensions of self-reported dispositional mindfulness. Psychological Assessment. 2016;**28**(7):803

[56] Choi E, Leroy H, Johnson A, Nguyen H. Flaws and all: How mindfulness reduces error hiding by enhancing authentic functioning. The Journal of Occupational Health Psychology. 2022;**27**(5):451-469

[57] Ramiller NC, Burton Swanson E. Mindfulness routines for innovating with information technology. Journal of Decision Systems. 2009;**18**(1):13-26

[58] Thatcher JB, Wright RT, Sun H, Zagenczyk TJ, Klein R. Mindfulness in information technology use: definitions, distinctions, and a new measure. MIS Quarterly. 2018;**42**(3):831-848

[59] Roberts KC, Danoff-Burg S. Mindfulness and health behaviors: is paying attention good for you. Journal of American College Health. 2010;**59**(3):165-173

[60] Sun H. Making sound adoption decisions: A longitudinal study of mindfulness in technology adoption and continued use. In: ICIS Proceedings. Vol. 2. 2011. pp. 1-20

[61] Carson SH, Langer EJ. Mindfulness and self-acceptance. Journal of Rational - Emotive and Cognitive - Behavior Therapy. 2006;**24**:29-43

[62] Hyland PK, Lee RA, Mills MJ. Mindfulness at work: a new approach to improving individual and organizational performance. Industrial and Organizational Psychology. 2015;**8**(4):576-602

[63] Chaskalson M, Hadley SG. Mindfulness: Historical and contemplative context and recent developments. In: Reb J, Atkins PWB, editors. Mindfulness in Organizations: Foundations, Research and Applications. Cambridge, United Kingdom: Cambridge University Press; 2015. pp. 42-66